834

"That we are
what we have
is perhaps the most basic
and powerful fact of
consumer behaviour."

—*Russell Belk, consumer behaviour researcher*

kidfluence

why kids today mean business

kidfluence

why kids today mean business

ANNE SUTHERLAND

BETH THOMPSON

McGraw-Hill Ryerson

Toronto   Montréal   Burr Ridge, IL   Dubuque, IA   Madison, WI   New York   San Francisco
St. Louis   Bangkok   Beijing   Bogotá   Caracas   Kuala Lumpur   Lisbon   London   Madrid
Mexico City   Milan   New Delhi   Santiago   Seoul   Singapore   Sydney   Taipei

McGraw-Hill
Ryerson Limited
A Subsidiary of The McGraw-Hill Companies

ISBN: 0-07-087133-7

1234567890 TRI 012345678901
Printed and bound in Canada.

Canadian Cataloguing in Publication Data

Sutherland, Anne, 1963–
    Kidfluence : why kids today mean business

Includes bibliographical references and index.
ISBN 0-07-087133-7

1. Child consumers. 2. Children—Social conditions.
I. Thompson, Beth. II. Title.

HC79.C6S97 2000   658.8'34'083   C00-932381-3

Publisher: **Joan Homewood**
Editorial Co-ordinator: **Catherine Leek**
Production Co-ordinator: **Susanne Penny**
Editor: **Lynn Schellenberg**
Interior Design and Page Composition: **Heidy Lawrance Associates**
Cover Design: **Zig**

To Andy—who had the idea that
I could do it
and
To Steve—who made
my own childhood so memorable

Table of Contents

Chapter 7: More Than Toys: An Overview of
Kids' Economic Impact // 91

The kid market is comprised of three components: the $115 billion North American market of kids with their own discretionary income, the $600 billion market they influence and the limitless market they will become in the future.

Chapter 8: Kids Buying Kid Stuff // 95

There are over 88 million kids in North America and they are spending money everyday. This new reality is transforming businesses from redefining traditional industries to the creation of completely new opportunities.

Chapter 9: Kids Influencing Family Purchases // 119

Kids' influence in the consumer world is expanding beyond purchases made solely for them. How they "nag" and how their parents respond to that plays an important role in family purchases including big-ticket items.

Chapter 10: Kids as Future Purchasers // 135

Around the age of 8 years, kids start recognizing brands more and making independent purchases. The brands they hold dear when they are young could be the brands they prefer as adults, making lifetime value and customer loyalty critical concepts.

Chapter 11: The Adults of Tomorrow // 157

Fast forward to 2015 when the bulk of Generation Y will be 25 years old. This generation has grown into adults with different characteristics than previous generations. They were raised in a prosperous and digital world. What effect will this have on their future?

Chapter 12: Coming Full Circle // 175

For the last several decades, boomers have been driving the change in our world. Now their reign is coming to an end. In the 21st century, it's the kids who are forging the way. They are what we must become.

Case Studies // 181

Preface

Anne Sutherland:
My business is to know people. My company, Planning Ahead, is hired by other companies to help them get to know their customers. All my business life I have worked on assignments that have involved kids and moms; from cereal to pasta to electronics and retailing to safety and recycling to face care. And regardless of the specifics of each situation there has always been one thing in common—kids and kid influence.

When I worked on a project for the Blue Box recycling program in 1990 we discovered that it was kids who made adults recycle. Kids learned the three Rs of recycling in school, brought that information home and pressured their parents. We learned that a public service message could not motivate adults to drag the blue box to the curb every week but they could be guilted into it by their kids. This insight changed how we communicated to parents and to kids. Parents listened to their kids and they acted on it.

As a strategic planner I spend my time talking to people to understand their motivations, needs and desires. Talking to kids in many different situations over the years has given me insight into their world. Planners, like anthropologists, observe and interpret. We conduct ethnographic research to uncover consumer behaviour patterns. In this role, over the years I needed to acquire an understanding of the stages of intellectual development in children in order to create advertising that appealed to kids six to 11.

I started to see what makes kids tick when I questioned them on how they nagged and cajoled their moms to choose the snacks they wanted, and then I had it quantified it in persuasion testing. I got a peek into the private world of teens when I watched young women wash their faces in their homes. I have asked kids to draw new super heroes to go on labels for canned pasta and asked teens to share lunch with me so I could watch them pour ketchup on their favourite foods. I have read dozens of books on kids, ranging from marketing "how to advertise to kids and teens" titles, to psychology and sociology texts on child development, to parenting manuals discussing "how to talk so kids will listen and listen so kids will talk." I have hung out with kids, read their magazines, watched their shows and shopped with them.

I also know their parents; many of my clients target moms and dads. Moms happen to be a specialty at Planning Ahead. We have interviewed hundreds of moms and have walls filled with secondary source information on moms and their families. We initiated a mom panel to keep in touch with moms across Canada, and we collect information for clients through our consulting and research division called Mombudsman. Beyond being a mom myself, these individual experiences over fifteen years have added up to a broader understanding of different kid age groups, their roles in their families and influence with their parents.

The idea for this book came about in a casual conversation I had with my husband, who had started to work with a new client, YTV, the kid television station. Andy was impressed with the quantitative information YTV had gathered over the years on the economic impact of the tween age group ("in between" ages nine and 14). YTV had gathered the statistics to demonstrate that tweens really did matter to business. Since Andy and I were both in marketing, we were intrigued by the future implications of these buying tweens. Sharing our different business experiences, we found our questions led to theories, and ideas started to take shape. Kids impact the economy. Kids grow up to become adult customers. Kids are big business today and will be tomorrow. The thesis of the book was born.

Beth Thompson:

As a journalist, I have been writing about Canadians for 20 years, most recently as corporate projects editor for Today's Parent Group. One such corporate project is a family lifestyle magazine called *Zellers Family*, which Anne and I have worked on together for a couple of years now.

As an editor, I sift through volumes of information everyday from national and international organizations that are eager to share their ideas, studies, statistics and new project start-ups. I hear about the latest gadgets, the newest technologies, the best way to teach kids things. I talk to parenting educators and experts regularly to help answer questions our readers have about living in the 21st century. My files bulge with information on families of all shapes and sizes.

In addition to editing *Zellers Family*, I am founding editor of *Today's Grandparent* and current editor of *Arthritis News*, both publications that deal with our Depression-era and aging boomer populations. Working on these two magazines has allowed me the opportunity to correspond weekly with a group of readers, who have a completely different set of aspirations and challenges than today's parents. I also edit a magazine called *Healthy Woman*, which focuses on health, wellness and relationship concerns during the teenage years, through the family years and beyond. It allows me the opportunity to keep in touch with many Canadian women, and to get a true sense of what their issues are. Past experiences—including contributing health and lifestyle writer for consumer magazines such as *Today's Parent, Canadian Family, Chatelaine, Canadian Living* and *HealthWatch*—combine with my current publishing ventures to provide me with a unique vantage point from which to observe the impact of change on today's families.

My interests in "kidfluence" run deeper than the fact that this is what I do for a living. As a mother of three boys aged seven to 12, I also deal daily with the reality of a changing society and the implications of that change in the lives of my children. As any parent does, I want to understand the world we live in so that ultimately I can make it a more interesting and rewarding place for my kids.

When Anne invited me to collaborate on *Kidfluence*, I jumped at the opportunity. The issues we talk about in the pages ahead are ones that I edit and write about on a regular basis.

Some of our own stories, both as kids and parents, appear here, as do those of parents we've interviewed. Where they have requested, we have changed their names.

We have found the growing world of kidfluence a fascinating and thought-provoking topic, and hope you do too. We would enjoy hearing from you. Be in touch with us at: www.kidfluence.com.

Acknowledgements

Thanks to our researchers Rhea Seymour, Kim Hacker, Michele Kiss, and Charlene Wildeman, whose tireless efforts to conduct interviews and track down statistics, study results, international data and permissions have made our job much easier.

Thanks to Zig. They brought us the idea for the book and we were lucky enough to have one of their talented art directors, Samantha McCormack, create the cover.

We'd also like to thank YTV for opening their survey results to us. Their ground-breaking Canadian research on kids and tweens first inspired this project.

We'd also like to thank everyone on the McGraw-Hill Ryerson team whose efforts went into this book, and a special thanks to Julia Woods for her vision and support.

Finally, thanks to the "guys"—Andy, Garrett, Rick, Jordan, Drew and Chad—for their unconditional support during the writing of *Kidfluence*.

Welcome to Kidfluence

I have seen the future, and it works.
—Lincoln Steffens

When it comes to children we have pure thoughts. Our North American culture encourages us to believe in kids. We see them as society's potential. We nurture and protect, guide and teach them. We want kids to be dreamers, believers, builders and creators. To borrow from Mark Twain, we give them roots, then wings, so that the rich and wonderful lessons of youth will foster courage and wisdom necessary to build the future.

As a society, we hold these ideals in high esteem. So why is it that kids are suddenly important not only to families, but to those who run the boardrooms of the nation? How is it that kids are flexing their economic muscle and getting results? Why are children having such an impact in today's world of adults?

A major reason is that kids mean big business. Boasting a spending power of $115 billion they are influencing their families and businesses in new ways and to an unprecedented degree.

Also there are more of them. We are experiencing a new generation of 8 million Canadian kids under the age of 20. Looking at North America as a whole, they number 88 million strong. Born between 1980 and 1999 this generation is the largest since the Baby Boom. They comprise 26 per cent of the Canadian population and, just as with their boomer parents, their presence is being felt in all aspects of life.

This new cohort answers to a variety of names: **Generation Y**, a natural since they were born after Gen X; the **Echo**, since they are children born of boomer parents; the **Net Gen**, since they are the first kids to enjoy technological privileges such as the Internet; and the **Millenials** since they are growing up at the turn of the century.

Like their parents, these kids live in a consumer culture. To a degree never seen before, they are judged by the clothes they wear just as we are judged by the cars we drive. They are growing up with adults who are encouraged to identify with branded consumer choices, who see themselves as part of the "Pepsi Generation" or the "Real Thing." Most adults don't make things or grow things or even repair things much any more. We buy. Our time-pressured lives encourage us to buy things just for the convenience. So our kids grow up seeing the ubiquity of our consuming ways and respond to it in a natural way. They too want "more." The end result? Generation Y kids have a voice, they know what they like, what they want, and how to get it.

But this book isn't just about kids as consumers. Their influence is much greater than their own considerable spending power. Just how great is their influence? And how have they come to wield such power?

In the first half of our book, we discuss how today's kids have come to be at the decision-making table. We look at how the boomers' more inclusive family philosophy has given previously unseen influence to the children and resulted in new consumer implications in many business categories. We explore the idea of the adultification of youth—a phenomenon that sees kids "getting older younger" due to a variety of influences such as involvement in sports at a younger age and earlier onset of puberty. We also discuss the influences of multiculturalism, mass media, and technology on kids. Throughout, we observe the impact of prosperity in kids' lives.

The second half of *Kidfluence* shares the findings of many experts who have studied the economic impact of kids, not only through their own spending, but also through their influence on the purchases of their family. We look in depth at three kids' markets—what kids buy for themselves, how they impact their parents' purchases and their significance as future grown-up consumers.

Kidfluence is about kids who are in control. Not out of control. Not in someone else's control. But kids who control more of their destiny today than possibly at any other time in history.

In conclusion, we show you that as the world progresses, kids today are exactly what and where they need to be to deal with the realities of the 21st century. Like most journeys we find ourselves coming full circle in the end. Kidfluence starts by considering the role society thinks kids play and ends with the very surprising role they actually do play.

Kid Control. Kid Power. Kid Money. =
Kidfluence on the rest of the world.

1

Looking Back: 20th Century Parents and Kids

Nothing endures but change.
—Heraclitus

To understand the present we need to know something of the past. This is true of everything in life, from academics, to politics, to social movements. So it is with this book—to really have a sense of today's kids, we need to know how families have been acting, and reacting, to life around them in the years gone by. Of course, there are volumes of data written about each subject we will be tackling. We have focused predominantly on the 20th century and, in every instance, we have looked for the most relevant and the most interesting data that will help you get an easy handle on the issues of the time.

The Way We Were

Are kids today growing up too quickly, being forced to become adults ahead of schedule? It's not a new thought. If you could have peeked inside the mud cottages and castles of yesteryear, you'd have seen that for centuries the youngest members of society were not distinguished from their older counterparts. Instead, children were thought of simply as smaller versions of adults. In medieval times, historians note, there were virtually no differences between children and their parents—from what they wore, to where they worked, to how they spoke, their lives were identical. And so it was for hundreds of years.

"Children were expected to participate in the household economy almost as soon as they could walk. They worked more or less as servants," says Steven Kline, professor of communications at Simon Fraser University in Burnaby, B.C., and contributor to Henry Jenkins's *The Children's Culture Reader* (New York Univeristy Press, 1998), a book that examines the roles of children throughout history. "The whole community shared work and leisure as well as games, songs and tales."

If we fast-forward a couple of centuries, we see changes occurring. The first is that as the adult world broadened to include reading and other intellectual pursuits that children were incapable of participating in, distinctions between young and old became more defined. The second is that as adults become more concerned with children's safety, children were taken out of the adult working world (mines and factories), and thus no longer viewed as simply apprentices, born to learn or carry on a family skill or craft.

According to Kline, "During the 19th century a powerful idea came to prevail as the dominant view of child development: that children are innocent beings in need of formation and learning, to be protected from the harsher realities of industrial society."

Both church and state became advocates for children during these times and big supporters of education for the young. "The new mission for childhood was to become literate, numerate and well-behaved," explains Kline.

Through that century and into the 20th, schooling took on greater importance. "It was at school, after all, that children would derive their first sense of their position in the broader social matrix of jobs, civic duty, social responsibility and moral choices," comments Kline.

It was also around this time that the concept "play is the work of childhood" was born. And, as Kline notes, so too was a whole new industry: "The Victorian awakening to the preciousness of childhood helped ensure that children's goods would expand along with other markets."

This brief look back in time shows how the role of children evolves and adapts to fit the current thinking of the day. It's not that the nature of children changes so much, but that their role is amended to fit society's needs. This was never truer than in the 20th century.

The Age of Change: The 20th Century

No other era in the history of the world experienced as much change as that which went on between 1900 and 1999. At both ends of this hundred-year period people experienced monumental events: automation transformed the start of it, technology revolutionized the end of it. Sandwiched in the middle was a world trying to adapt and advance in the face of constant newness and considerable upheaval. The world was in serious turmoil for the first half of the century; two world wars and the Great Depression wreaked havoc in North America on and off over a 31-year span from 1914 to 1945.

Throughout this book, we refer often to different 20th-century generations—a generation being a group of people defined by their dates of birth. Our focus begins with the G.I. Generation (1912–1921), the Depression Generation (1922–1927) and the Silent Generation (1928–1945). See Figure 1 for at-a-glance generational information.

The life experiences gained throughout the first half of the century moulded the fundamental beliefs of Canada's youth at the time which spanned the G.I., Depression and Silent generations. They learned early on that working long hours and making constant sacrifices were absolutely necessary to over-

Children, American Style

In North America, there were additional influences that spurred change. According to Karin Calvert, another contributor to *The Children's Culture Reader*, Americans saw youth as an advantage. "Although the same sorts of changes were happening in England and in parts of Europe, youth took on special meaning in America. Americans of the Revolutionary era and of the new republic had become accustomed to a new political rhetoric in which America was the child colony or the young country, as opposed to the overbearing mother country. The advantage lay with youth and vigour."

FIGURE 1: *A Look at the Generations in Canada*

Generation* Dates	GI 1912–1921	Depression 1922–1927	Silent 1928–1945	Boomers 1946–1965	Generation X 1966–1979	Generation Y 1980–1999
Pop. in 1999	872.0	1,780.0	3,876.1	9,510.0	6,532.4	7,996.9
% Pop. in 1999	3%	6%	13%	31%	21%	26%
Shared Experience	Scarred by depression—self-denial lasts a lifetime. First generation of contemporary media.	Coming of age in the 40's they shared a common enemy and a common goal.	Born to late to serve in war. Benefitted from post war growth and social tranquility.	Social upheaval lead to determination to change the world and desire to experience it all.	Scandals and scares make X uncertain. First generation to experience widespread divorce.	Live in longest boom market. Greatest time of technological change. Mass Media and consumerism integral part of life.
Money Philosphy	*Save for a rainy day*	*Save a lot, Spend a little*	*Save some, Spend some*	*Spend, Borrow, Spend*	*Spend? Save? What?*	*Spend. More. More. Spend.*

*Generations calculated to closest StatsCan age breaks, 1999.

Source: *Content adapted from "Making Generational Marketing Come of Age" Fortune, June 26, 1995, Faye Rice.*

come the general adversity of the times. Margaret Anderson (G.I. Generation), whose father worked for Simpson's department store in downtown Toronto, remembers that her father, together with other employees, was asked by the company to buy Simpson's shares with his weekly earnings. "We could barely afford it, but it was expected. This type of loyalty was predominant then. You worked hard and you were loyal to your company; it was what you did. There was reciprocity though. Companies believed in their employees, unlike today where people seem more dispensable to corporations. My father never lost his job throughout the Depression or War Years," she remembers.

Of course, many others were not as fortunate, including her future husband's family who lost much of their life savings in the 1929 stock market crash. Remembered John Anderson, who was eight at the time, "As kids, we were afraid, but didn't dare ask questions. It wasn't our place to worry about that, yet those dark years had an impact on every facet of our youth."

As a result, the life lessons were hard-learned and long-lived. Some 70 years later, a great many of this generation still clip coupons, refuse to make long-distance calls during daylight hours and rarely make a major purchase without great justification and the cash to back their transaction. "It's bred in your bone," Margaret says simply. "I could buy a $200 dress now, but I never would. I could get three perfectly good dresses for the price of one!"

This generation was a group of people who, for the most part, deeply respected authority.

What's a Cohort?

Beyond generational dates there is a phenomenon called cohorts. Cohorts are determined by important external events that occur during a generation's formative years. For example, those most affected by the Depression were the G.I. generation born between 1912–1921 because they were adults during the Depression, an experience that shaped their lasting life attitudes. It is your cohort that determines what memories you share with other people. Woodstock is often used as a marker for the boomer generation but it is only a memory for the early boomers because the late boomers born from 1955 to 1966 would have no collective memory of the Woodstock experience.

(Continued on next page)

What's a Cohort?
(Continued from previous page)

The echo boom's cohort experience will be dominated by those at the peak of the boom born around 1990. These kids are 10 years old in the year 2000. They will be united by their memories of the turn of the millennium, such as watching the midnight celebrations around the world on their televisions. It is their stories and points of view that set the stage for the new world of kidfluence.

You can read more about cohorts and generations in the books *Rocking the Ages—The Yankelovich Report on Generational Marketing*, and *Generations* by Neil Howe and William Strauss.

Of course, every nation has its movers and shakers who lead the way for social change and growth, and Canada was no exception. We had our share of mavericks and movements (Christian Reform and the Suffragette movement at the turn of the 20th century spring to mind) but generally speaking, it was *very Canadian* to conform to the status quo, to follow the rules set out by government.

In 1939, as Canadians headed to war, the country relied on its government to get them through. Margaret Anderson, then 20 and "promised" to a bomber pilot who never made it back, remembers: "We *had* to look to the government for guidance and inspiration, especially in matters of the war or the world. They had the information, the facts to make decisions. We didn't have access to that kind of information ourselves. Global news was slow in coming and rumours were always rampant about what was happening overseas. We needed someone to believe in, to trust in."

Respect for authority lingered well after the war years in many aspects of life both small and large. Ruth Scott of the Silent Generation remembers that you "dressed" for your doctor's appointment, and that you accepted, without question, what your children's teacher told you about your own kids. "The line was drawn, and unless you were extremely well-educated or very well-connected, you didn't cross it."

It was a comfortable way to live, to put your trust in others in difficult times, and the payoff was good. Both the Silent and Depression generations went on to become the first Canadians to enjoy unprecedented economic stability, even prosperity, in the post-war years. It's no wonder, then, that they raised their families the same way: with strict rules and prudent spending habits. With a tumultuous half-century behind them, parents were relieved and happy to play it safe. Their children, knowing no other way, obediently followed suit.

The annual family holiday offers a microcosmic glimpse into family life at the time. "I remember that my parents carefully budgeted and planned our annual two-week summer break," one boomer tells us. "We usually rented a cottage up north, at a lake. As kids, we were advised of, but *never* consulted about, such decisions. Truth is, we never expected to be asked. We were just happy at the prospect of such an indulgence, regardless of the venue."

The Boomers' New Outlook

During the second half of the century, Canada experienced unparalleled growth—9.5 million children were born between 1945 and 1966. Dubbed the baby boomers, the sheer magnitude of this cohort has been responsible for great change across our country and others.

There is so much about this generation that differed from the preceding one. Rites of passage familiar to all humans—falling in and out of love, making babies and burying parents—often played out in vastly different order for the pre-boomer generations. Then, young lovers may never have had the chance to fall *out* of love, or may have buried parents 30 or 40 years prematurely. As we found from talking to people who grew up during the war years, many of their basic beliefs were formed as a direct result of the strife around them.

Experiences shared collectively shape the culture of the time. This is evident when comparing boomers and their parents. While the youth and young adulthood of the boomers' parents were coloured by economic and personal struggle, boomers knew nothing but stability. Thus, boomers have always had an innate sense of comfort and ease, a contentment their parents would never allow themselves, regardless of their eventual financial standing or material well-being.

It is not hard to understand, then, how the boomer generation grew up to be so self-assured and confident. Life was good in Canada whether one was an early or late boomer. There was no threat of wars or drafts that other countries were experiencing—a fact that didn't go unnoticed to about 30,000 Americans who dodged the Vietnam draft by officially immigrating to Canada. (It's generally assumed that at least that many more came unofficially.)

Technology was welcomed into households across the nation, making life easier (first with automatic washing machines and then automatic dishwashers) and more enjoyable (television sets and custom-built stereo systems). Post-secondary education was no longer considered a privilege for a few but a right for many. According to data from the Association of Universities and Colleges of Canada (AUCC), enrolment began to inch upwards in the early 1960s, not levelling off until the early 1990s. In a 1999 report entitled *Trends: The Canadian University in Profile*, the AUCC writes, "In Canada, full-time enrolment between 1960 and 1975 grew more strongly than in the U.S." (see Figure 2). The U.S. has long been regarded as the leader in making university education accessible.

It was this same cocoon of stability and comfort, however, that ultimately bred a restlessness in the early boomers, the post-war youth. They wanted to make their mark, to prove their coming of age, to protest perceived injustices. The generation that had it all began to speak out on behalf of those who didn't. They vented their anger at the very institution their parents had trusted above all others to see them through tough times—the government. The anti-establishment backlash in Canada echoed the larger protest movement south of the border. Later-born boomers embraced the same ideals as their older siblings, especially the concept of a more individualistic society.

FIGURE 2: *University Enrolment in Canada*

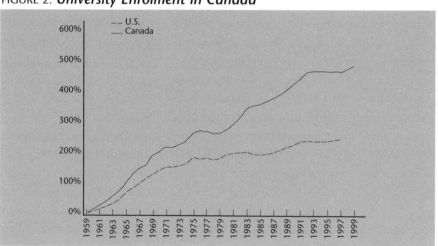

Source: *Trends: The Canadian University in Profile, AUCC, 1999*

The boomers have made their mark. In general, we have less respect for institutions today, and more desire for promoting individualism than did previous generations, writes Michael Adams in his book *Sex in the Snow: Canadian Social Values at the End of the Millennium*. As you can see by Figure 3, the trend toward distrusting Canadian institutions is high.

These changes began happening in the early 1970s when the idea took root that more than a chosen few should speak for the majority. In the U.S., government began shifting from a representative democracy to a more participatory democracy. John Naisbitt, who became known in the 1980s as a leading future-trend reporter with the book *Megatrends* said in that book: "The guiding principle of this participatory democracy is that people must be part of the process of arriving at decisions that affect their lives....People must feel that they have 'ownership' in a decision if they are to support it with any enthusiasm."

Similar trends were being charted north of the 49th parallel. Municipalities across the country began holding plebiscites on issues as diverse as fluoridation in a town's drinking water to establishing new electoral boundaries. It wasn't long before this ideology filtered into other aspects of life. It just made sense to confer with those close to you about decisions that would ultimately affect them. And so began a whole new era.

FIGURE 3: *Canadians' Confidence in Their Institutions*

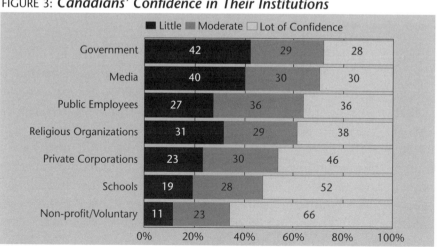

Source: *Ekos Research Associates Inc. Rethinking Government 1998*

The Boomers Have Kids—or Not!

When boomers turned their thoughts to settling down and raising a family, they once again had a huge advantage over their parents. With the advent of oral contraceptives, introduced in the early 1960s, family planning became a reality. Children were no longer just something that came along nine months after the honeymoon. Now couples had an active role in determining when, or even *if*, to start procreating. Whereas three or more kids was the average number of children for the G.I., Depression and Silent generations, David Foot, author of *Boom, Bust and Echo* says the average boomer family had fewer than two kids. Figures 4 and 5 show how the average family size is declining in Canada. Notice, too, that women have consistently been choosing to have their children later in life. Recent data from Statistics Canada continues to support this trend (Figure 6). By 1996, 31 per cent of first births were to women over 30, compared to only 12 per cent back in 1951.

FIGURE 4: *Canadian Families [1] are Shrinking in Average Size*

	Number in Thousands	Average Size
1971	5,042.6	3.7
1981	6,309.2	3.3
1991	7,482.1	3.1
1998	8,116.9	3.1

1   Excluding the Yukon and the Northwest Territories.

Source: *Statistics Canada, Catalogue no. 91-213-XPB, 1996.*

Boomers with Babies

For the first time since the dawn of civilization, parenthood became a choice. The ramifications were far-reaching. Says Dr. André Lalonde, Executive Vice-President of the Society of Obstetricians and Gynaecologists of Canada, "The advent of the Pill was the most significant event for women's health in the last 100 years. Not only did it free women from the burden of unwanted pregnancy but was an important cure for many serious menstrual health problems. For the first time in history a couple could separate the biologic function of reproduction from sexual enjoyment and pleasure. In the end, the Pill gave every woman freedom to reach her own true potential." And it gave every couple freedom to choose when to become parents. So parenthood took on added meaning

FIGURE 5: *Family Changes: More Single Kids Today*

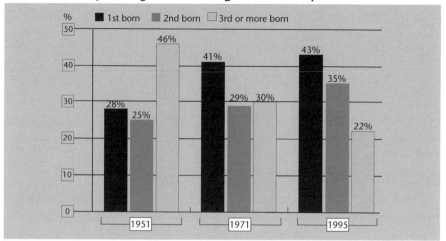

Source: *Statistics Canada, Canadian Social Trends, Winter 1995, and Births and Deaths 1995, Catalogue 84-210-X1B*

—couples embraced the news of pregnancy because it was something they planned for.

New latitudes and attitudes became the order of the day. Boomers felt very comfortable exploring new parenting ideas and relished the opportunity to put them into practice. Ann Douglas, a mother of four and author of nine books including *The Complete Idiot's Guide to Canada in the '60s, '70s and '80s*, notes that women especially began to flourish; marriage didn't automatically mean a life sentence of children and chores. The 1970 Royal Commission on the Status of Women confirmed to Canadians that children were everyone's responsibility—both parents' and society's in general—and that women had the right to work outside the home.

"At the start of the 1960s, Canadian women had yet to make significant inroads into the workforce. While it was acceptable for childless

FIGURE 6: *Mothers Are Older*

	1st Birth	**2nd Birth**
1972	23.1	25.6
1982	24.6	27.1
1992	26.6	29.0

Source: *Statistics Canada, Catalogue no. 91-213-XPB, 1996.*

FIGURE 7: *Kids on the Rise Again in Canada*

Children's Age	1971 (end of Boom)	1981	1991	1999 (all Gen Y)
0–4	1,816.2	1,783.3	1,953.2	1,831.0
5–9	2,254.0	1,777.0	1,952.9	2,067.3
10–14	2,310.7	1,921.0	1,913.0	2,032.0
15–19	2,114.4	2,314.9	1,925.9	2,066.6
Total 0–19	8,495.3	7,796.5	7,745.0	7,996.9

Source: Statistics Canada, 1999, 1991, 1981, 1971

married women—or women with school-aged children—to work outside the home, society had grave reservations about having mothers of preschoolers holding down jobs in the paid labour force. Consequently, it wasn't until well into the 1970s that it became commonplace for women with preschoolers to work outside the home," says Douglas.

It was during the 1970s, of course, that the first boomer kids were becoming parents of preschoolers. Thus, along with bringing new creativity to their role as parents, boomers undertook the task of rebuilding the very foundations of the traditional family model. The now-tired idea of authoritative rule gave way to a fresher, more contemporary concept of democratic rule. Words such as choice, openness and permissiveness worked their way into the lingo of parenting. More freedom in the family structure—from choosing when to become parents, to choosing whether or not to stay home and raise the children—ultimately led to more freedom in family attitudes.

Some of these changing parenting sensibilities were reinforced by the thinking of Dr. Benjamin Spock, the American pediatrician who wrote *Baby and Child Care* (originally *The Common Sense Book of Baby and Child Care*) in 1946. This book was revolutionary in several ways. It was one of the first parenting advice books available, and Dr. Spock deviated from what were considered the norms of the day. He encouraged parents to be flexible, to trust their own common sense and to be more affectionate and respectful of their kids. It took many years for his ideas to firmly take root in Canada; not many kids raised in the 1950s remember parents following the doctor's orders. His philosophies were a better fit with boomer parents, and they continue to be popular.

With over 50 million copies published in about 40 languages, some estimates put *Baby and Child Care* second only in sales to the Bible. Dr. Spock may have been the first of the permissive parenting advocates, but he was certainly not the last. By the mid 1980s, two other childcare experts, British psychologist Dr. Penelope Leach and U.S. pediatrician Dr. T. Berry Brazelton, were also best-selling authors in the child-rearing book market. Today, theirs are but a few of the hundreds of instructional tomes bursting from the library shelves, ready to help parents better raise their families. Of course, each one comes with its own set of ideas and philosophies, offering new opportunities and child-rearing choices. Whereas boomers' parents would never have ventured far from the beaten track—never felt the need to—today's parents (the middle- to back-end of the boomer cohort) are constantly being tempted with "new and improved" models to explore.

Even though Generation Y (the eight million children born 1980–99) is smaller than the boomer generation, when you add the explosion of parenting material to the fact that it was affecting millions of kids, it's easy to understand how ideas such as permissive parenting quickly became trends. The sheer number of

Dr. Spock inspired fresh thinking for parents.

people hungry for information means an idea has less time to incubate before demands bring it to the world stage. So, children began to live the change their parents eagerly embraced.

The New Status of Children
A major transformation directly attributable to new parenting ideals was that the child's status was irrefutably elevated in the household. New dynamics began to develop within family circles, one of the most notable being the shift in the balance of power.

Instead of parents making all the decisions, more bi-directional relationships began to develop—where parents and kids influenced each other. Such relationships create more give and take in the family circle and offer all members the chance to learn and grow through each other, says Donna Lero, co-director of the

THINK OF THE OLD FAMILY MODEL AS AN INVERTED TRIANGLE WHERE PARENTS SET RULES AND MADE DECISIONS AND KIDS FOLLOW.

Centre for Families, Work and Well-Being at the University of Guelph in Guelph, Ontario.

In the new family model, kids feel like a valuable part of the family unit and grow up believing they have the right to vote on all issues affecting their family, including purchasing decisions. Small questions like "What should we get Grandma for her birthday?" to weightier queries like "Where shall we spend our summer vacation?" are within the parameters of normal dialogue for most families.

THINK OF THE NEW FAMILY MODEL AS A CIRCLE. PARENTS STILL RULE, BUT DECISION-MAKING BECOMES MORE DEMOCRATIC. CHILDREN ARE NO LONGER EXPECTED TO BLINDLY FOLLOW ALONG, BUT ARE ENCOURAGED TO PARTICIPATE IN DISCUSSIONS.

In fact, today's parents go as far as to say it is unfair not to include younger members of the family in buying decisions. Families who do not confer with their children about purchases, either of a daily nature or larger one-time acquisitions, deny their kids an opportunity to develop important life skills.

Many families who have adopted these democratic practices like the dignity they give the family. They promote the concept that all family members are equally valued and given consideration regardless of age; a concept that is part of permissive parenting. That's an ideal older generations sometimes view negatively. To them, permissive means you have no control over your children, that you are too lenient. Permissive parents have young children who yell in restaurants, have no manners and jump on Grandma's couch even when they've been told not to. Permissive parents let their teens stay out late and have parties while they're away. How can permissiveness ever lead to anything worthwhile?

But if you look up the word permissive in *Webster's Dictionary* you'll find definitions like "tolerant" and "allowing discretion." Boomers identified early with these positive connotations of the word because it fit their mindset. A permissive parent is, by extension, a more tolerant and flexible individual. As a tolerant parent, you take the time to understand your child's point of view. As a liberal parent you encourage your child's self-expression. Permissive adults make for a more child-friendly world where kids are allowed to be kids and are not required to adapt to grown-up standards. Permissive parenting offers children the opportunity to grow in new and dynamic ways, to become confident and self-assured adults.

These parenting ideas are still with us, says Holly Bennett, who, as editorial director of Today's Parent Group, has been observing parenting trends for more than a decade now, but she notes that the labels are changing. Bennett says the term permissiveness has lost its positive connotation, even among parents who are.

In some circles, she says, permissive has come to mean "unable to set any limits at all." Though Dr. Spock, who had respect for parents as well as their children, would be surprised at this take on his kind and gentle revolution.

Another way to describe this type of parenting might be to call it, simply, liberal. "Effective, liberal parenting is not abdication of the parent's responsibility to provide safety, care, guidance and standards of behaviour," says Bennett. "It's not 'yeah, whatever' parenting. It's more like a commitment to provide this guidance in a way that respects the child's personal integrity, and that encourages/allows the child to make or participate in decisions in an age-appropriate way."

It's an idea Bennett explored in-depth with co-author John Hoffman in a March 1998 *Today's Parent* article called "Under My Thumb.": "Parent-child relationships have changed. Today's parents tend to be less authoritarian, more flexible and more willing to consider their child's point of view, a trend that has grown gradually over the last few generations. Ethically, it has great appeal: It feels like moral progress to extend the 'golden rule' to our relationships with children, as well as other adults."

Democratic Dad

Boomer dad Aubrey Ferguson of Oakville, Ontario, believes it is critical for his daughter to be included in decision-making processes. "Inclusion in the discussion and rationale of a purchase, then in the actual shopping and negotiating (if there is any), is development of an essential life skill. The sooner it is learned, understood, practised and mastered the better it is for the child as she matures and takes on responsibility for her life." Ferguson encourages his daughter to express her opinions when the family is shopping for groceries, planning an evening of entertainment, or looking at future vacations.

They did ask the big question, as have other trend-watchers: has the pendulum swung too far? Have parents lost their authority? Ultimately, they don't think so, but maybe some ideas are in need of tweaking, says Vancouver parenting educator and president of Parenting Today, Kathy Lynn. "I don't use the word 'democratic' with respect to parenting because that implies everyone has an equal vote and that misunderstanding gets parents into trouble. I prefer to say 'co-operative.' In a co-operative family, we all participate at the level of our competence and the level of our responsibility."

That's a theory that fits with today's realities. The parents we interviewed believe it's important to give their children a voice, but then they weigh that input against the importance of the decision. For instance, a 10-year-old may get the final choice about which cereal he gets for breakfast, but most parents are not looking to him to make a decision about whether to buy a minivan or SUV. Parents may invite their children's discussion in debating the merits of one vehicle over another, but only after they've narrowed down their choices to two or three cars that interest them. The kids' enthusiasm for a certain feature (captains' chairs in the backseat of a minivan) will play a role in influencing the parents' decision, but ultimately, it is still the parents' decision.

In Search of Eternal Youth

The shift in the balance of power between parents and their kids is also directly attributable to the boomers' desire for preserving their youthfulness. Boomers want to be young and stay young and one way to do that is through their children. Instead of shunning kids' fashions and culture as parents of yesterday did (think of the collective disdain over the likes of Elvis, bellbottoms and sit-ins) today's adults embrace their kids' youthfulness and want to understand it, be a part of it. When cargo pants became fashionable for kids, parents wanted them too; when kids started rollerblading and snowboarding, parents asked their kids to teach them how. It's more important to this group of middle-agers to stay youthful than it was for their counterparts at any other time in history.

According to Peggy Edwards, Miroslava Lhotsky, and Judy Turner, the authors of *The Healthy Boomer: A No-Nonsense Midlife Health Guide for Women and Men*, "Growing up in the 1960s and 1970s led us to believe that a long, healthy, affluent, and youthful life was our birthright.

Midlife is a shock." In our effort to combat this change of life, we search out a healthier lifestyle, often taking part in activities normally associated with a much younger crowd. For instance, in the 1998 Boston Marathon more than 50 per cent of the runners were over 40, they write. The authors note that both men and women will "go to great lengths to try to avoid the realities of aging."

Connecting with kids takes on a whole new meaning as boomers fight to hold on to their youth.

SPEED READ SUMMARY

- The influential role kids play in today's family decision-making is not something that occurred overnight, but a trend that has evolved over the last 40 years. Children react to the world around them—to the beliefs of their parents and to the opportunities placed before them. This is true of all generations.
- The cohorts known as G.I. (1912–1921) and Depression (1922–1927) were frugal and conscientious about consumption, having survived financial disaster and two world wars.

- The Silent Generation (1928–1945) trusted authority figures as more worldly and knowledgeable. They raised their children with authoritative rule and an eye to prudent spending.
- The Boomer Generation (1946–1966) was the first group to have real contraceptive options, making parenting a choice, not an inevitability. They have enjoyed stability and economic comfort. Interested in permissiveness and a participatory democracy, they rewrote family and social ideologies.
- Boomers brought kids to the decision-making table.

2

Today's Families: Variations on a Theme

The family is the nucleus of civilization.
—*Will Durant*

It is not a coincidence that the political, economic and sociological events of the 20th century dramatically affected and altered family life as it was known. We can see that today's children are a product of their environment, just as their ancestors were. Their grandparents were forever influenced by tumultuous decades of war and depression and their parents were indubitably shaped by the post-war boom years.

We may have started out with the very Victorian principle that children should be seen and not heard, but we ended up at the polar opposite of that motto. Today's children play an integral and vital role both in our family and in society as a whole. To fully understand that role, we must look beyond the exterior world and peer inside to the very core of the family itself. In this chapter, we introduce you to a number of Canadian families as well as to several experts in children's mental health for their interpretation of the changing role of children within the family model.

Like an intricately assembled glass mosaic where the individual pieces create the contrast, depth and beauty of the final art form, the diversity of today's families defines our country in the 21st century. For starters, we are much more an urban demographic than rural (see Figure 1), so much so that in just over 100 years we have completely reversed the trend of urban/rural living. But even more than where we live, *how* we live today has the greatest impact on our world. From dual-income partners to single parents, from blended families to multigenerational ones, each contributes to society in its own way. By looking individually at the various family settings and the dynamics within them, we get a better grasp of the shifting status of the child in his family environment.

FIGURE 1: *Canada is an Urban Country*

	Urban Population (%)	Rural Population (%)
1871	18	82
1931	50	50
1971	76	24
1991	77	23

Source: *Statistics Canada, 1999.*

Dual-Income Families

The number of families where both parents work outside the home is steadily climbing. In fact, it more than doubled in the last quarter century alone, according to Statistics Canada. In 1970, there were 1.9 million families with two working parents and by 1995 that number had jumped to 4 million.

There's no doubt that when both parents work, family dynamics are altered. What spurs the most change is obvious: dual-income parents are less able to spend time with their families. A recent StatsCan survey indicates that working parents have less time for their family than just six years before. Men aged 25–44 spent an average of 5.6 hours a day with family, while women managed slightly more at 6.1 hours.

Time-strapped parents look for ways to compensate for this lack of togetherness. Often this means that children's desires take precedence over parents' wishes when it comes to entertainment or eating out.

Veronica Devries, a mother of two teenaged girls, has worked outside the home since her daughters were babies and stresses the importance of quality time. "If our time together is limited, I don't want to go to a restaurant where they won't eat, or take them somewhere where they're going to be miserable. We want our kids to be happy, so we involve them in the decisions." It is an attitude expressed again and again: family time is too precious a commodity to make the decision how to spend it without input from the whole gang. Kids' opinions count.

Dr. Dan Acuff, author of *What Kids Buy and Why*, and president of Youth Market Systems Consulting in the U.S., calls this new attitude "filiarchy." In the December 1999 article "Play Dough" featured in *American Demographics*, he explains that the power shift is directly attributable to having less quality time together. "We've gone from a patriarchy, to a matriarchy to a filiarchy, where [a lot of] power is ceded to the kids. It's whatever you want, Johnny."

Parents today value their kids' opinions and take them into consideration when making decisions that effect the whole family.

Guilt has a strong role to play in the new dynamic, says Dr. Freda Martin, a child psychiatrist and director of the Hincks-Dellcrest Centre for Children's Mental Health, and an associate professor of psychiatry at the University of Toronto. "As parents have less time to spend with [kids] they replace time with material things. Meeting a child's needs materially may be more of a bargaining process today. Parents may try to win their affection with material things." If a parent feels lousy because he can't spend the time he wants to with his child, he can lessen his pangs of regret and guilt by buying the child a much-sought-after toy or treat. The purchase is directly influenced by the child's desire.

"Dual-income couples are exchanging stuff for time," agrees Clair Hawes, a West Vancouver psychologist, who runs a mental health clinic that services families across the social sphere. Parents, too, acknowledge guilt as a reason for letting their kids influence purchase decisions, but they tend to put it lower on the list. Moms and dads put a more positive spin on the role of kids' influence in their dual-income lives: When there's more money coming in, more can go out. "More income means more leeway to give in to kids' urgings and preferences," said a mother of two, Rosalyn Wosnick, while a dad, Aubrey Ferguson, echoed with, "Dual incomes mean we are able to consider and respond to our child's input."

With 70 per cent of moms now working outside the home according to StatsCan, more Canadians see family time slipping away, and the working parents' struggle to balance home and work life seems to be getting more difficult. The StatsCan *General Social Survey on Time Use*, reports that the "struggle to juggle" in 1998 left more people feeling they did not have enough family time compared with those polled in 1992. One in three people was dissatisfied with the lack of balance in his or her life, a situation felt most acutely by married parents aged 25–44 who were working full-time. Paid work and work-related activities increased by two hours a week over the last six years for both parents; men averaging 48.6 hours and woman 38.8 hours. Adding to the strain is the fact that unpaid work responsibilities (household work, childcare, shopping, volunteerism) have also increased by 30 minutes a week since 1992 with woman clocking in at 34.4 hours, men at 22.8 hours.

What do these numbers add up to? A squeeze play for time. An almost universal example revolves around juggling the morning routine. Those few hours after everyone's out of bed and before everyone's out the door tend to be the most hectic for families. Consequently, there's little time to be arguing over who's eating what for breakfast. It's much simpler to let the children make their own choices about what juice and cereal they want to buy at the grocery store. Once again, this gives children some power in family decisions they may not have had a generation before. "It used to be that Mom went to the store, brought home what she brought home, and you ate what she served you," says Dr. Acuff. "Today 72 per cent of food and beverage purchases are influenced by kids."

Single-Parent Families

When it comes to the time squeeze, probably no one feels the pinch more than single working parents who now make up 22 per cent of the population, according to StatsCan. In the same struggle-to-juggle survey, data show that single-parent mothers spend more hours at work (both outside and inside the home) than any other group. Interestingly, however, there are some parallels with the dual-working parents. For instance, StatsCan shows them neck and neck for least amount of leisure time: 3.6 hours a day when averaged over an entire week. And single mothers are as determined as two-parent families to include children in decision-making. "Virtually any items or plans that affect them, I involve them in," says Jane Silver, mother of two boys. "It's their life, too."

But it is the prominent *difference* between these two groups that accounts for a notable elevation of the child in the family: the lack of a second adult in the daily routine.

"I find I often turn to my daughter in situations where I would likely have first turned to a partner," single mom Donna Phillips told us. It's human nature to suss out opinions from those around us before we make a decision, significant or otherwise. Lone parents feel compelled to check it out with the kids first, says Phillips. Herself a daughter of a divorce, she says childhood memories motivate her to include her daughter in decision-making. "I felt so vulnerable as a child because I was never included in my mother's decision-making."

Single-parents households are more democratic than traditional family settings, says child psychotherapist Janet Morrison, who is a psychological associate in private practice in Toronto, treating children, adolescents and adults. "In single- parent families, even if the adults are not marshalling the kids in their war against each other and elevating them that way, they just do rely on them more for emotional support; it becomes more democratic, the lines of power are fuzzier."

In talking to families, we have found that the level of responsibility increases for the children of single parents, but the amount depends on how old the kids are when the situation arises. Chris Stewart, who was left a widow with three children when her husband died in a car accident, says the dynamics in their household changed virtually overnight. Her 17-year-old son became the "man of the house," and his 14-year-old sister took on more responsibilities cooking, cleaning and caring for her younger, six-year-old brother. "The older kids have had to grow up in a hurry," says Stewart wistfully. "We work constantly to fill the void in our lives, but even with the kids taking on so much extra around the house, we come up short. Four people are not five, no matter how you do the math."

Morrison has seen situations like Stewart's in her practice and agrees. "When a father dies, what's the mom going to do? The whole authority

Joint custody is a growing trend in Canada. In 1997, 24 per cent of parents had joint custody of their children after divorce, up from 13 per cent in 1991 and 21 per cent in 1995.

structure shifts in these cases—because it *has* to." But just as they are expected to shoulder more of the household chores, children are also invited to participate in more decision-making. This is true of many of the single-parents we spoke with. For instance, if older siblings have to get dinner started or babysit younger brothers and sisters after school, it seems logical that parents consult them on these issues—What after-school snacks to buy, what movie to rent, and so on.

Some single parents move in another direction. One woman we interviewed, who was widowed when her two children were both under five, says she consciously took responsibility away from them so they wouldn't have to assume adult worries at an early age.

There are important similarities among one-parent families, however, that are worth noting. While some single parents may not want to give their kids extra duties and others do, one dynamic all single-parent families seemed to share is a sense of camaraderie, of equality, between adults and kids. One mom described it as an "us against the world" spirit that shielded them from the outside craziness when necessary.

Blended Families

With remarriage, family life is dramatically altered for children who must adjust to shifting roles, often on the fly. The list of change is endless: there is a new parent, perhaps new step-siblings, different styles of parenting, new rules, probably a new home and additional sets of grandparents, to name a few things. From a child's perspective, if both parents remarry or take up residence with new partners, the change grows exponentially. And, if there are step-siblings, chances are a child's place in the family is also altered.

In Canada, such scenarios are playing out constantly in living rooms across the country, says the Vanier Institute of the Family, a non-profit organization based in Ottawa. In its book *Profiling Canada's Families II*, it says the number of remarriages doubled between 1970 and 1989, from 29,975 to 62,276. Although the remarriage rate has fallen in the 1990s (more people are now simply living together), the Institute says about two-thirds of single parents can be expected to either marry again or cohabit.

In kidfluence terms, a parent's remarriage means family dynamics, and the child's role within that unit, change. "I've done a lot of work with reconstituting families and there are huge issues," says Morrison. One of the most workable solutions is to elevate the child and include them in the discussions. "Kids hate change, we all do. Kids are an integral part of the family unit and for the new dynamic to work, they have to be allowed to talk about it," Morrison says.

There's no doubt that many kids whose parents have been involved in divorce and remarriage are exposed to an adult world much sooner than previous generations. Many kids know more about their economic situation than their moms and dads ever knew (or know!) about their parents. This is partly due to the fact that money affairs come up frequently during the merging families' negotiations. Stretched for private time, adults often discuss such matters in front of the children. Divorce heightens this reality when kids hear conversations about supporting and managing two or more households.

The flip side is that parents *want* to include kids in their conversations. When everything else is changing in their lives, some parents work hard to keep kids in the loop, hoping it will smooth the transition of change and keep things familiar. Says Linda McCarthy, whose children were 14, 13 and 12 when she remarried: "We tried to include the kids in family decisions, so as not to cause resentment, but also insisted that they participate responsibly and bring an excellent attitude to the table."

At a consuming level, the changes resulting from a blended family are also sharp. Consider the five-year-old child who suddenly has an 11-year-old sister. Almost overnight she is exposed to a new and much older world. At an exaggerated pace, her consuming interests move from baby dolls to Britney Spears; from playing house to playing video games. To a younger child, the older world seems so much more exciting. If there is shared custody, another reality is that the child who has one of everything may suddenly need two—one for each house she lives in/visits.

Divorced parents often buy more material objects for their children as a way of easing guilt.

For parents feeling culpable for causing upheaval in their kids' lives—or for new parents trying to make friends with a child—new toys or fun getaways are not out of the picture. Like the guilt-wracked working parents who fear they aren't spending enough time as a family, some parents concerned about the effects of family restructuring may try to keep their kids happy with material things.

A more positive spin on this indulgence, as McCarthy points out after years of struggling on her own, is that a double income family can be a welcome relief. "Two paycheques created a whole new lifestyle for my children and our move up to a century home with three cars on the road alleviated the financial problems the four of us had previously experienced."

Multi-generational Living

Living arrangements that include grandparents or grandchildren as part of the standard family unit are certainly not new. Aging parents have long being invited to move in with their children, especially after their spouse has died. But there is a twist: boomers who delayed child-

FIGURE 2: *Who's Living with Whom*

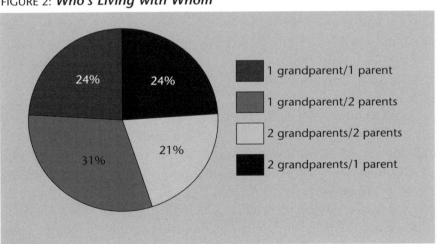

Note: Third generation always present.
Source: *Statistics Canada, 1996 Census of Population*

bearing until their late 30s and early 40s are now finding themselves caught between two life phases, caring for their young children at one end, and their elderly parents at the other. Those dealing with this situation have been dubbed the Sandwich Generation, and it's a trend that will burgeon. In the past decade the number of three-generation households has increased 39 per cent—from 150,000 in 1986 to 208,000 in 1996. See Figure 2 showing the various living arrangements of three-generation families.

Almost one in three Canadians is now a grandparent. It's a fast-growing segment of our population for two reasons. One, improved health care and nutrition mean that seniors are living longer than ever before, and two, the boomers are now becoming grandparents—the average age of today's grandparent is 59.

When grandparents live with their families, many of them contribute money to the household income, resulting in higher average family incomes: $66,000 vs. $57,000, according to the summer 1999 report of *Canadian Social Trends*. (See Figure 3) Even though per capita income is lower due to more people in the household, when resources are pooled to allow for economies of scale, it has the effect of raising the standard of living, the reports says.

FIGURE 3: **Grandparents in House Means More Money in House**

	Three-generation Households	
	No.	%
Total households	208,500	100
Number of income recipients in the household		
	No.	%
None	35	1
One	2,800	0
Two	36,620	18
Three	77,905	37
More than three	91,100	44

Note: Numbers may not add to 100 due to rounding.
Source: *Canadian Social Trends, Summer 1999, based on 1996 Census of Population, Statistics Canada*

When the conditions are right, children can benefit greatly from having grandparents live with them. Donna Taurasi, who straddles the line as a boomer in a more traditional cultural setting—her aging in-laws moved from Italy in 1992 to be closer to them—says her children have blossomed with self-assurance and confidence living with their grandparents. "It's made them better people. They have a sense of culture, of tradition," she says of her daughter and son, who were nine and 14, respectively, at the time of their grandparents' move. But more than that she notices that her kids have a deeper respect, not only for their grandparents but also for her and her husband. "The kids see what we do for our parents, how we help them. It gives them a broader sense of responsibility."

Grandparents have their own relationship with kids. They elevate them, indulge them, make them feel special. Parents may fall back on yelling at their kids, but grandparents can step back and see the bigger picture, or both sides of the story. "Sometimes," says Taurasi, "it means the grandparents get through to the kids easier than I can."

Psychotherapist Morrison has seen this positive side through her work. "I think kids can benefit tremendously from having their grandparents around. They can be very supportive of the child and wonderful allies." But she's also dealt with the downside. If the grandparents are ill or financially burdened, then it can be very difficult for the family, especially the children. And, sometimes, when the family becomes "top-heavy" the children can lose autonomy. "It all depends on how the Sandwich Generation parents accept the situation. If Mom and Dad are resentful and annoyed, it's hard. It's also hard if it happens later [when the kids are older] rather than earlier."

Sometimes it's hard not to be resentful, especially for women. According to a 1994 report from the Vanier Institute titled *Profiling Canada's Families*, women spend about twice as much time caring for elderly relatives as men do. In one study, they

> **85 per cent of married moms** (aged 25–44) who work full-time said weekdays were too short to accomplish their goals, as did 79 per cent of dads, in a 1998 StatsCan survey on juggling time. About 50 per cent of this group said that given more time, their first priority would be to spend more time with family and friends.

reported, women giving care to older family members missed an average of 35 hours of work per year, nearly a full week, on that account. One in five thought about quitting work entirely due to their caregiving responsibilities. In another study, one in three caregivers had either quit or adjusted her job to fit with her responsibilities for older family members.

Taurasi is one of many women living this reality and agrees that there *are* negative aspects to deal with. But she also believes that in terms of making kids' lives rich in outlook and understanding, "the positives far outweigh the negatives."

The Impact of Change

Once again we see that children respond to and evolve in relation to the world and, more specifically, the family around them. It gives us pause to ask: As we stand on the cusp of the 21st century, in which direction will we move?

If half of all marriages now end in divorce, if 70 per cent of all families have dual-income parents, if remarriage is on the rise, that means children are more often exposed to changing family dynamics, to situations where parents turn to kids more frequently for decision-making, for emotional support and for friendship.

Is it possible we are headed once more toward an integrated world, where as in days of old, the lines between childhood and adulthood blur?

Of course, it's not that simple. It's true that as the adult world gets busier and more complicated children get handed more responsibility and play an increasingly elevated role in the family. But, on the other hand, society is doing a good job—maybe even a *better* job than in previous years—at protecting our youth, at cherishing their childhood.

Organizations have been developed whose sole purpose it is to elevate the health and well-being of children. One such group, the Canadian Institute of Child Health, based in Ottawa, runs a program called The First Years Last Forever, which aims to educate all parents on the critical importance of the early years of life.

There are other areas where efforts are obvious. Children are constantly reminded that they have rights, for example, that no one is allowed to touch them without their permission; definitely a first in our society. Children have been taught that they are the boss when it comes to their bodies, which gives many of them confidence to respond to what they deem unsuitable, whether an approach from a stranger or a hug from Mom they simply aren't in the mood for. There are other indications of society's growing desire to protect children and childhood:

- Most provinces have bicycle helmet laws in place.
- Many provinces offer standardized school testing to ensure kids in different areas receive the same level of education.
- Breakfast clubs are in place across the country to give kids a nutritious start to the day.
- Police nationwide host car-seat clinics to make sure parents secure children properly.
- Corporations raise funds annually to send underprivileged children to camp.
- Society has seen and responded to the need for places like Ronald McDonald House, which offer ailing children and their families a respite from gruelling hospital routines.

What starts out sounding like a mixed message—grow up faster/preserve youth—actually reflects an evolutionary step toward achieving a balance. Yes, we are calling on children to do more and be more, but at the same time we are investing in their youth, building their self-esteem in new ways. The world is moving faster, but society is working harder to carve out a special place for kids in order to make the most of childhood.

SPEED READ SUMMARY

Changes in family structures and attitudes during the last half of the century figure prominently in raising kids' level of influence.

- *Dual-income families* doubled from 1970 to 1995 from 1.9 to 4 million people. More discretionary income allows parents to accommodate kids' preferences. Families short on time acquiesce to kids' desires more frequently.

- *Single-parent families* have grown to account for 22 per cent of all households. Kids are invited to participate in decision-making because they are more involved in running the household. Absence of a second adult means decision-making shifts toward kids.

- *Blended families*, which include remarriages and multi-generational living, are on the rise. In remarriage, familial inclusion is key to successful reconstitution. In multi-generational living, kids learn responsibility and are indulged by grandparents.

- Society has a growing desire to invest in kids, to help build their self-esteem in new ways, which leads to kids becoming an even stronger influence.

3

Modern-Day
Experiences of Kids

Experience is not what happens to you.
It is what you do with what happens to you.
—Aldous Huxley

Without a doubt, the trip through childhood takes less time in 2001 than it did a generation ago. Is the road getting shorter or are today's kids moving faster? It's probably a little of both. To some extent, kids have always been in a hurry to grow up, to enjoy the freedom and glamour they see as part of the territory. A 1998 survey conducted by Toronto-based polling firm Environics Youth Research Division (YRD) found that 12- to 14-year-olds want to be 18, while 15- to 19-year-olds want to be 20. "Typically, young people aspire to be a few years older than they actually are, a fact that has important implications for marketing to them," the YRD survey says. "What to adults may appear as precocity and presumption, to teens may appear as simply being treated as mature equals."

The challenge for most kids has been how to gain access to that older realm. From the Victorian age on, the world has worked diligently to create a separate and nurturing space for children. But we're losing sight of that long-held ideal. Today, the road through childhood is cluttered with signposts offering shortcuts to the age of majority. And one shortcut seems to lead to another so that before we know it, kids have arrived at their destination ahead of schedule.

There are actually a number of contributors to the adultification of youth, from the very obvious, *technology*—which we explore in greater detail in subsequent chapters—to the barely perceptible, *evolving attitudes*. In the following pages, we will look at the many and varied components—access to information/technology, organized sports and other structure, earlier physical development, multiculturalism and travel—that contribute to the maturing process.

An Explosion of Technology and Information

To really appreciate how vastly different today's kids are, one has to understand how accustomed they are to the modern conveniences that technology affords. Following is an abbreviated 1999 version of a list Ron Nief and Richard Miller of Beloit College in Wisconsin develop annually to give faculty a sense of the mindset of the First Year students in the class of 2002, (who would be born in the early 1980s):

- They have always had an answering machine.
- Most have never seen a TV set with only 13 channels, nor have they seen a black-and-white TV.
- They have always had cable.
- There have always been VCRs, but they have no idea what BETA is.
- They cannot fathom not having a remote control.
- They were born the year that the Walkman was introduced by Sony.
- Atari predates them, as do vinyl albums.
- The expression "you sound like a broken record" means nothing to them.
- They may have never heard of an eight-track tape. The Compact Disc was introduced when they were one year old.

- Popcorn has always been cooked in the microwave.
- They don't have a clue how to use a typewriter.

Imagine the attitudes of kids one decade from now, who'll believe personal computers are a fixture at home, or at least a school standard, and that money has always come out of the "magic money machine" in the wall at the bank. Children of today don't think twice about having instant access to unfathomable amounts of global information through the Internet. Even three-year-olds know how to turn on computers and can speak in dot com.

If you stop to think about the wave of experience that these kids are riding, it is nothing short of remarkable. The explosion of technology has most notably resulted in an explosion of information. Consider the following:

- There has been more information produced in the last 30 years than in the previous 5,000.
- It has been said that today's *Sunday New York Times* contains a greater volume of information than an Englishman from the 1700s would have been exposed to in a lifetime.
- The information supply available to us doubles every five years.

This accelerated pace of disseminating information means kids are more aware of the world around them; everywhere they turn news is revealed to them, on TV, the car radio, the Internet. "Kids are learning more at a younger age because of the media age," says Donna Lero of the Centre for Families, Work and Well-Being in Guelph. "They're exposed to more and aren't pro-tected from the real world of adults any more in many families."

Lero says this early exposure gives parents a chance to talk about decisions with kids and allows opportunity for new dialogue to take place within the family. But even more than allowing for new dialogue, this unending supply of informa-tion allows today's kids to look at things in a completely different light than did previous gener-ations. For starters, the world is a much smaller place, making events much more relevant and personal. CNN's coverage of starving families in Third World countries evokes a genuine human response in today's

> Aided by technology young kids have a heightened awareness of the world around them.

children, as opposed to the blank stares given mothers of yore who told their kids to "eat your vegetables, children are starving in Africa."

Through mass media kids today have a greater sense of possibility. "Kids are exposed to both great examples and sad examples. One day they hear about Columbine, the high-school shooting, and the next how a 17-year-old created and sold an Internet company for a million dollars," says a group of employees at the NRG group, a Toronto-based business "incubator" and youth-marketing service. "Young people hear about young people doing great things and that will empower them to do great things, which will empower them again—it's all a big circle."

Of all the possibilities the new information frontier holds, the most exciting is the reality of this equation: limitless information equals limitless potential. Lack of technological know-how may have delayed or curtailed fulfillment of an idea in the past, but with modern technological advances occurring at the speed of light, kids get the message that all things are possible—if not today then definitely tomorrow.

KAGOY (Kids Are Getting Older Younger)

This access to limitless information and its accelerated pace of dissemination not only affects children but their parents too. In fact, it plays a significant role in what's called KAGOY.

When we think of children growing up faster our minds flash to those on the brink of puberty, seeing images of nine-year-old girls wearing lipstick or 10-year-old boys in trendy street wear. But KAGOY actually begins much sooner than that and in a more altruistic form. Parents, in the hopes of giving their child a head start in life, are now reading and playing music to their unborn babies. Such ideas are inspired by recent research on the brain that has become fodder for every parenting magazine around the world. The basic premise is that early stimulation wires a child's brain for life. Human brains are composed of trillions of neurons that need to be used in order to become a functioning part of the complex circuitry of the brain. The earlier children learn, the more neuronal connections will develop and the smarter, more self-assured the children will become. Figure 1 shows where and when there is potential for "learning windows." Armed with this information, parents leap into action. Realizing they can play a

FIGURE 1: *Early Stimulation can Wire Kid's Brains for Life*

Each skill has a different "learning window" in the brain.

THE LOGICAL BRAIN	THE LANGUAGE BRAIN	THE MUSICAL BRAIN
SKILL: Math and logic	SKILL: Language	SKILL: Music
LEARNING WINDOW: Birth to 4 years	LEARNING WINDOW: Birth to 10 years	LEARNING WINDOW: 3 to 10 years
WHAT WE KNOW: Circuits for math reside in the brain's cortex, near those for music. Toddlers taught simple concepts, like one and many, do better in math. Music lessons may help develop spatial skills.	WHAT WE KNOW: Circuits in the auditory cortex, representing the sounds that form words, are wired by the age of 1. The more words a child hears by 2, the larger her vocabulary will grow. Hearing problems can impair the ability to match sounds to letters.	WHAT WE KNOW: String players have a larger area of their sensory cortex dedicated to the fingering digits on their left hand. Few concert-level performers begin playing later than the age of 10. It is much harder to learn an instrument as an adult.
WHAT WE CAN DO ABOUT IT: Play counting games with a toddler. Have him set the table to learn one-to-one relationships—one plate, one fork per person. And, to hedge your bets, turn on a Mozart CD.	WHAT WE CAN DO ABOUT IT: Talk to your child—a lot. If you want her to master a second language, introduce it by the age of 10. Protect hearing by treating ear infections promptly.	WHAT WE CAN DO ABOUT IT: Sing songs with children. Play structured, melodic music. If a child shows any musical aptitude or interest, get an instrument into her hand early.

Source: *"Your Child's Brain," Sharon Begley, Newsweek, Inc., February 19, 1996.*

vital role in maximizing their children's potential, they are no longer content to sit idly by and let nature take its course. From Mozart *in utero* to flashcards in preschool, the push to succeed, to grow, to mature begins earlier than ever.

One of the first industries to pick up on KAGOY was the toy market. A New York-based market research firm called The NPD Group noted serious lows in retail sales among traditional toys such as dolls, games and puzzles during the 1999 Christmas season, says Simon Ashdown of *KidScreen*. During that same year, The NPD Group noted an even more startling trend. In one study they conducted they found "kids were moving out of the categories of dolls and action figures at age six—a year-and-a-half to two years earlier than they did a decade ago."

Sports and Structure

Ashdown notes in *KidScreen* that KAGOY is also found in traditional childhood pursuits such as sports. Says Richard Leonard, vice president of the Zandl Group, a New York City market research company which specializes in trends research with the under-30 consumer: "What you have today is a lot of aggressive baby-boomer parents, who are pressing their children to excel at and enter into activities like organized sports and summer camp—things that, traditionally, kids have started at a later age." This over-activity has created the "alpha child," says Leonard, a miniature adult who is too busy to play with toys. This alpha child is spending less time just playing today than two decades ago, according to a study by researchers at the University of Michigan. *The Panel Study on Income Dynamics, Child Development Supplement* reported that kids under 12 in 1981 played in unstructured play and outdoor activities for 30 minutes more than kids studied in 1997. Overall free-time which was 40 percent of a kid's day in 1981 accounted for only 25 per cent in 1997.

These opinions describe a North American trend many others have been witnessing in ball parks and hockey arenas continent-wide. Rick Campbell, a former newspaper sports editor and minor sports coach in a southwestern Ontario city for 20 years, says organizations have been making it easier for younger children to become involved in team play. T-ball is a perfect example. The sport is relatively new, introduced to Canada about 30 years ago as a variation of baseball. Because it eliminates the pitching element—kids hit the ball off a flexible tee-stand at home plate—players as young as five can get involved. Now, cropping up in cities across Canada and the U.S., is something called *pre*-T-ball. According to the T-Ball USA Web site, this game is for kids as young as three and a half. It's marketed as an opportunity to teach them the fundamentals, hitting and running to a base. "By the very nature of the game, trying to capture and keep their attention is well nigh impossible. In general, kids' motor skills just aren't that refined. Structure at this age seems not only peculiar, but excessive," Campbell comments.

The same trends are noted in hockey. When Campbell began covering minor sports in the late 1970s, he remembers that "parents thought it was cute to watch seven-year-olds chase a puck haphazardly around the ice. They laughed and the kids had fun." But over the course of his career, he noticed changes. Adults were no longer laughing with the kids, but yelling at them to "play their system." "In a very short period of time, it effectively went from a game of shinny, to an institutionalized approach where systems and responsibilities are over-emphasized at a too-young age," says Campbell.

We need to keep sports fun, emphasizes Dr. Barry McPherson, author of *The Social Significance of Sport* and architect of an Ontario government-commissioned report on minor hockey in the early 1980s. "It should be a part of a kid's life, but not something that consumes him. When hockey is viewed as a child's leisure activity, it can be a wonderful experience, and that's how we should view it."

There is recognition of this fact on a grander scale and a lament for the loss of the fun of sport. In his book *The Disappearance of Childhood*, American communications theorist and former editor of *Et Cetera*, the journal of general semantics, author Neil Postman writes: "Except for the inner city, where games are still under the control of the youths who play them, the games of American youth have become increasingly official, mock-professional, and extremely serious."

A result of all this, he writes, is the early entry of kids into professional sports. "Twelve-year-old swimmers, skaters, and gymnasts of world-class ability are commonplace. Why is this happening? The most obvious answer is that better coaching and training techniques have made it possible for children to attain adult-level competence." The corollary, of course, is that in some sports it is not inconceivable that a 14-year-old Olympian is washed up at the ripe old age of 20.

Back to Basics

We may soon see a return to more fun and creativity in sport. During the winter months of 2000, the Canadian Hockey Association hosted the Molson Open Ice Summit, which tabled a report that included 11 recommendations for minor hockey. Among the recommendations were the following, which emphasized the importance of both fun and skill.

- Ensure that coaches are trained to reward and encourage a child's use of creativity and imagination.
- Expand the implementation and marketing of the Initiation Program (designed to introduce children to hockey with an emphasis on FUN and skill development).

The full report can be found on-line at www.canadian-hockey.ca/openice/e/index.html

It is interesting to note that Postman wrote those words about 20 years ago. They are still true today; we are still on the same fast track and sports enthusiasts like Campbell think that's a shame. "I played organized sports like hockey, but not until I was about nine. My fondest memories are not of organized sport, but of the nightly ball-hockey games on our street, when you could dream of scoring the game-winning goal or making the game-saving stop and you'd play until dark—or until your mother called you in for dinner."

It's not just in sports that this trend to structured activities is being noticed. The adult world of organization and formula is pervading many aspects of kids' lives. When both parents work, it means toddlers are being signed up for preschool programs that are, out of necessity, very structured programs. According to *American Demographics*, children are home less now. "Overall, children ages three to 11 now spend about six hours a day in preschool or school, a two-hour increase since the early 80s," wrote Charles Fishman in a May 1999 article "The Sandwich Generation. "

Recent Canadian statistics are similar; Figure 2 shows that in 1994/95 40 per cent of the country's 2.3 million children under the age of 6 spent about 27 hours a week in child-care while parents worked or studied.

And, during summer months, many kids move from one kind of classroom to another: camp. It all sounds fun—tennis camp, circus camp, hockey camp—but once again, it's a very structured setup, where children are introduced to new ideas, dynamics and challenges earlier than before. Structure, it seems, has become an inevitable part of

FIGURE 2: **Who's Watching the Kids (1994/1995)**

12% – Parent(s) not employed or studying

40% – In non-parental care arrangements while parents hold job or study

48% – No supplemental care used

Source: *Statistics Canada,* National Longitudinal Survey of Children and Youth, *reprinted from the Vanier Institute of the Family, 2000.*

life in the 21st century and a major contributor to the KAGOY phenomenon.

Hitting Puberty Earlier

Children, most notably girls, today are experiencing the first signs of puberty almost a full year earlier than a mere half-century ago. These startling facts come from the American Academy of Pediatrics (AAP) which recently published a study on early puberty after analyzing data gathered from over 17,000 U.S. girls. The study was led by Dr. Marcia Herman-Giddens from the Department of Maternal and Child Health, School of Public Health and the Office of the Chief Medical Examiner at the University of North Carolina, Chapel Hill.

Among her findings was the fact the average age for breast development in African-American girls is now 8.87, and 9.96 for Caucasians. While there is not a lot of comparative data available, one small study from 1948 that looked at onset of puberty in Caucasian girls found a mean age of development to be 10.8; a 1969 study was even later at 11.2.

FIGURE 3 **Sampling of 20th Century Studies: Girls Maturing Earlier**

Year	Subjects	Age Range	Mean Age Breast Development	Mean Age First Period
1948	49	8-18	10.8	12.9
1969	192	8 and up	11.2	13.5
1997	17,077	3-12	9.96	12.8

Source: *Figures are from American Academy of Pediatrics, 1997*

Couch Potato Kids

Earlier puberty in children can be linked to obesity, which in turn is associated with sedentary lifestyles. According to Andrea Grantham, of the Canadian Association for Health, Physical Education, Recreation and Dance, children spend about 26 hours a week sitting at school. Add to that the time they sit watching TV, playing on the computer or reading and you see sedentary habits being set early. It's a problem that will likely grow as education cutbacks force many school to offer less physical education. Data from the U.S. show that from 1965 to 1980 obesity in kids rose 54 per cent for six to 11-year-olds and 39 per cent for 12 to 17-year-olds.

Earlier puberty is a real phenomenon, says Dr. Herman-Giddens, that leaves many unanswerable questions. Fifty years hence will eight-year-old girls be getting their periods, and nine-year-old boys dealing with cracking voices? "I do not know where it will all end," Dr. Herman-Giddens admits, "but it is certainly concerning."

As *Kidfluence* was going to press, a study from Bristol University in the U.K. was just being released which also confirmed these new trends. In this study, 1,500 children were followed from birth. The results showed that one in six girls is now beginning puberty at eight compared with one in 100 a generation ago as is one in 14 boys at age eight compared to one in 150 in his father's day.

At this point, medical science can only speculate as to why girls may be physically maturing earlier. (No similar studies have been conducted on boys.) There are hormones, especially estrogen, in today's animal products, which may spur growth. And some hair products, including some shampoos, contain estrogen or placenta, which may also play a role. "Endocrine disrupters in the environment and hormones in the food are one theory, but I suspect that the answer—if it is ever found—will be a combination of factors," says Dr. Herman-Giddens. "Certainly one cause is the ever increasing proportion of obese children. Obesity is well-known to be associated with earlier puberty in girls."

Does physical maturity affect emotional growth? Most experts will tell you no. "There is no evidence to support [the suggestion that] children's emotional or cognitive abilities are more advanced just because their body's physical development is," says Dr. Herman-Giddens. "This is but one problem with early sexual maturity." In her AAP report she concludes that "the timing and content of sex education programs in schools may need revision."

U.S. psychologist Ava Siegler, author of *The Essential Guide to the New Adolescence*, agrees. "Preteens in our culture are 8 and 9. We shouldn't wait to talk to them about AIDS, sex and violence until they are 12," she says in a *New York Times* article "The Face of Teenage Sex Grows Younger" (April 2, 2000). That same article shows that in the last half of the 20th century, teenagers engaged in sexual intercourse at earlier and earlier ages. (See Figure 4.)

FIGURE 4 *Number of 15-year-olds Having Intercourse*

Early 1970s		Early 1997
Less than 5%	Girls	38%
20%	Boys	45%

Source: *National Center on Addiction and Substance Abuse*

Earlier sex education classes may be a good start to dealing with this development. But there's another angle to earlier maturation that is less easy to solve. While the North American world seems to fast-track childhood on the one hand, on the other, it also prolongs kids' from dependence on their parents. Society's hunger for knowledge has created a world with an ever-increasing need for higher education. This in turn necessitates a longer adolescence because children are more financially and physically dependent on their parents. This is especially true among girls, who just happen to be the kids hitting puberty earlier. According to *Trends: The Can-adian University in Profile*, a report produced in 1999 by the Association of Universities and Colleges of Canada, women now "make up more than half of all university students and account for more than 75 percent of enrolment growth over the past 15 years."

Earlier puberty makes it more difficult to acquire a balance between emotional and physical growth.

Surviving the tumultuous teen years is never easy, and the thought that children, certainly girls, may be reaching puberty faster, and living through adolescence longer, is unsettling. If earlier physical puberty is the new reality, is there any way to help children develop their emotional and mental growth as well?

It's not that simple, says Toronto child psychotherapist Dr. Janet Morrison, who is a psychological associate in private practice in Toronto, treating children, adolescents and adults. The idea that one could accelerate emotional development to match physical growth is dangerous. "A huge number of variables interact in kids' emotional and mental development, you can't take specific steps to maturity."

Finding a balance is key, she says. "We don't want to alienate a child by putting the lid on too tightly, or allowing them too much exposure too early." Parents need to let children enjoy childhood and work on building close, loving and trusting relationships with each other. This, in turn, will go a long way to augmenting emotional maturity.

The Influences of Multiculturalism

Cultural diversity is at an all-time high in Canada. Recent data from Citizenship and Immigration Canada shows that of 216,039 immigrants in 1997, 49,236 (almost 25 per cent) were children under the age of 14.

Exposure to different cultures enriches today's youth in untold ways. Curiosity, open-mindedness and tolerance, all of which are encouraged by an influx of new citizens with different perspectives, are invaluable traits to develop early, especially considering tomorrow's leaders will require a comprehensive global vision as the economic world shrinks to accommodate broadband technology.

On a day-to-day basis, kids enjoy the many benefits of living in a racially diverse society. One boomer mom relates the story of how her kids love to watch their Italian babysitter crush her own tomatoes every fall, following a time-honoured family tradition that dates back to the "old country". And, even though they celebrate Christmas, her kids hum along to Hanukkah songs, respect the solemnity of their Jewish friends' Yom Kippur and are keenly interested in finding out which animal will represent the Chinese new year. The opposite is also true. "We have shared many of our French-Canadian customs with Guyanese friends to the delight and wonderment of their children," she says.

The world will enjoy more long-term benefits of racial and cultural diversity—well-adjusted children who can easily adapt to a variety of situations. Judith Rich Harris tells us in her book *The Nurture Assumption: Why Children Turn Out the Way They Do,* "Children develop different selves, different personas, in different environments." Most kids have two environments, home and the world outside of home, and they behave differently in each. Harris, a former writer of college textbooks on child development, uses the example of a Polish family learning a new language, English, to illustrate this point: "It is common for immigrant children to use their first language at home and their second language outside the home. Give them a year in the new country and they are switching back and forth between their two languages... Step out of the house—click on English. Go back in the house—click on Polish. Psycholinguists call it code-switching."

It's Not Always About Sex

According to the 11th Annual Special Teen Report—a yearly survey conducted by *USA Today* of 272,400 teens, 16% of teens said they felt very pressured to "look a certain way." This category evoked higher responses than did other commonly associated teen pressures such as:

Having sex: 9%

Smoking: 8%

Using drugs or alcohol: 7%

Eager to distinguish the two environments and keen to be like their peers, children can eventually learn to speak a new language without an accent, even though they continue to speak Polish at home, even though their parents never lose their accent.

Harris later writes: "Childhood and adolescence are when people acquire the patterns of behaviour, and the inner thoughts and feelings that accompany these patterns, that will serve them for the rest of their lives."

If we take these views and apply them to the culturally diverse society we live in, interesting concepts develop. Imagine a generation of kids who can live comfortably in more than one world, in more than one culture, with more than one language? Then imagine the possibilities open to them in a grown-up version of that world.

Have Kids, Will Travel

In the 1800s a person rarely travelled more than 30 miles from the village they were born in; some kids now travel that far to daycare every morning. Thanks to their boomer parents, kids now enjoy travel opportunities—beyond the trip to the daycare—that previous generations could only experience through textbooks, post-university trips or by going off to war. Through firsthand experience travelling with their families, today's children are developing cross-cultural literacy. From an early age, travel has opened their eyes and exposed their minds to different values, customs, trends and standards of living, providing an insight into the world that is impossible to get in other ways.

Now, it's not unusual for kids to take cruises or to fly at very young ages. One boomer's mother commented on her daughter's family travels with her baby son. At the age of 18 months, the grandson had been to Florida three times and she, the grandmother, at the age of 60, was enjoying her first visit.

In previous generations, trips were mostly family visits to stay with relatives or friends. Pleasure flights were unheard of for middle-class Canadians. Many a boomer can remember cross-country road trips during school vacation to visit their parents' families, stopping along the way to visit other friends and relatives. Families camped, or stayed in motel cottages, picnicking by day at the side of the road. Eating out of the cooler wasn't about saving money, highway restaurants just didn't exist in the 1960s and 70s. Vacations were simple, not really educational, and virtually unchanged from year to year.

Bilingualism Boosts Esteem

A study reported in the *Journal of Social Issues* says that kids studying second languages in school immersion programs are enriched by the experience. Study co-author Professor Fred Genesee of McGill University in Montreal noted that kids in bilingual programs are more tolerant toward minorities, and have better social skills and self-esteem. "[These programs] provide students with the communication skills and cultural awareness that facilitates intergroup contact," thus reducing the chances of continuing discrimination issues.

Today people still enjoy staying with relatives, but families are also looking for new ways to spend holiday time together. Grown-up boomers, the first generation to travel extensively for pleasure, believe in the importance of exposing their children to experiences similar to those they've enjoyed. According to StatsCan, boomers represent the largest share of travellers within Canada, with the average age being 41. Canada Tourism refers to this cohort as "a widely educated and experienced traveller population."

Martha Chapman, manager of corporate communications, Signature Vacations, says there's a move toward focusing on travel as an educational experience for kids, rather than just an indulgence. Where previously there was an explosion of activity in June when school let out, now family travel is more evenly spaced across the calendar, says Chapman. She attributes part of this to a new attitude in schools. Teachers, many boomers themselves, understand the value of travelling and make allowances for kids to take trips during the year. "Kids can do a homework assignment related to their trip—create a trip diary or give a presentation about it upon their return," she says.

Over the last decade there's been a steady increase of children travelling abroad. In the seven years between 1990 and 1997, the number of kids under 12 who travelled outside of Canada and the U.S. jumped by 11 per cent. In 1997 alone, 1.1 million kids under 12 travelled outside of Canada, according to figures from StatsCan.

One 31-year-old Gen-Xer (the generation born 1965–1979) we talked to said that of the many advantages afforded his generation, the opportunity to travel has been the most beneficial. "Travelling tends to build confidence among young people. I had an easier time

Profile of a Traveller

According to the 1997 Canadian Travel Survey by Statistics Canada, education, income levels and domestic travel are linked.

"Although just 15 per cent of the population had a university degree in 1997, they accounted for 23 per cent of overnight (domestic) trips. In contrast, the 30 per cent of Canadians with less than a high school education accounted for just 18 per cent of the trips in 1997," according to StatsCan.

(Continued on next page)

**Profile of
a Traveller**
(Continued from previous page)

In 1997, those with a household income of more than $60,000 accounted for 37 per cent of trips, even though they only make up one-quarter of the population. "They stayed more frequently in hotels and cottages and, as they took more pleasure trips, stayed less with friends and relatives than Canadians with smaller incomes," StatsCan reports.

relating to new people and new situations at university, in part because of the level of diversity I had encountered travelling in foreign countries. In my own world I felt much more confident, less intimidated."

Chapman says that the growth of travel is related to the growth of two-income families in the last decade. "People are starting families later today so they're more financially comfortable by the time they have kids," she says. StatsCan backs that up. Its data shows those with household incomes over $60,000 are the ones doing the most travelling.

The reality of two working parents has had an impact on how vacation time is spent. Most hotels and resorts now provide kids' programs to attract the working parents looking for a real break. To parents who are desperate for downtime during their vacation, the idea of sitting poolside while their kids are entertained by the hotel equivalent of Julie the Cruise Director seems more appealing than a long drive to the lumpy bed at Aunt Marg's house. Add to that the fact that the children are making new friends with kids from other parts of the globe and the vacation value increases.

Travel does contribute a richness to youth in ways never previously imagined. This Gen-Xer summed it up best: "The day I stood at Checkpoint Charlie in Berlin, the year after the wall came down, I was filled with a new sense of purpose. I picked up some bits of concrete wall that had been chipped away by other tourists and I felt freedom in my hand. No book could teach me that."

SPEED READ SUMMARY

Kids have always been in a hurry to grow up—12 to 14-year-olds want to be 18, while 15- to 19-year-olds want to be 20—and today it seems that they're arriving at their destination ahead of schedule. There are a variety of contributors speeding them along:

- Technological advances. Thanks to the speed of technology, in the last 30 years there's been more information produced than in the previous 5,000.
- KAGOY—Kids Are Getting Older Younger. Parents read to unborn babies; competitive sports are introduced earlier, as boomer parents try to fast-track their children.
- Early physical maturity. Girls today experience first signs of puberty a year earlier than girls did a half-century ago.

- Cultural diversity. Multiculturalism is at an all-time high; recent stats show almost 25 per cent of immigrants are children. Sharing cultures and learning other languages brings depth and maturity to kids' lives.
- Travel. Since 1990 the number of kids under 12 who travelled internationally jumped by 11 per cent. These kids are enriched by experiences their parents had to wait until adulthood for.

4

The Wired World:
Its Impact on Kids

Knowledge is power.
—*Francis Bacon*

Two of the most influential vehicles driving change in the last half of the 20th century came via technological progress: TVs and personal computers. These wired wonders have played an integral role in elevating and empowering kids though they may bring new risks along with opportunity. This chapter explores the impact of TVs and PCs in kids' lives.

TV Times

It's helpful to look first at how much TV is being watched. According to a Kaiser Family Foundation (KFF) study, the typical American child spends 5.5 hours a day outside of school consuming media. The study, *Kids & Media @ The New Millennium*, defined media to include TV, computers, video games, movies, music and print. There were 3,000 kids involved, between the ages of two and 18.

Those 5.5 hours a day add up to a whopping 38.5 hours a week—the equivalent of a full-time job, said Drew Altman, Ph.D, President of the KFF. Canadian figures are even higher. While data are unavailable for combined media use, a 1997 StatsCan survey (see Figure 1) revealed that children aged two to 11 watched an average of 17.9 hours of TV a week (2.56 hours a day), while teens aged 12 to 17 watched an average of 16.9 hours weekly (2.41 hours a day). That combines for an overall daily average of 2.48, fractionally higher than the KFF findings of 2.46.

FIGURE 1: *Canadian Snapshot of TV Viewing (Fall '98)*

	Total	2–11	12–17	Men 18+	Womens 18+
			Hours Per Week		
Canada					
Total	22.3	16.6	15.9	21.4	26.4
Quebec					
Total	25.5	17.0	16.6	24.1	30.4
English	21.5	18.1	18.7	19.1	25.7
French	26.2	18.1	18.7	24.9	31.3

Source: *Statistics Canada, Catalogue no. 87F0006XIB.*

If you grew up in the 1950s, '60s or even the '70s, TV was considered a luxury activity, a nice way to spend a night with the family, but not something you did all evening, every evening. The TV programs were designed with both adults and kids in mind: "The Ed Sullivan Show," "Flipper," "Lassie," "Little House on the Prairie" and "The Brady Bunch" are good examples. Families gathered together in the living room for TV appointments—it's Sunday at six so it must be time for "The Wonderful World of Disney."

Today, the TV is on for more than scheduled appointments. And when Mom and Dad do sit down with the kids to watch a program, chances are the shows are more adult-themed than family-based. In the 1960s when an episode of "The Dick Van Dyke Show" was on, you knew what to expect: the language would be clean and the story line benign enough for the youngest family members. Today, TV is more of a crap shoot. Inconsistency in story lines makes it hard to find appropriate family viewing. Take "Friends," for instance. One week you might get a funny episode about Chandler trying to impress his boss, a clean story line with no swearing or overt sexual energy. But tune in the following week and you'll likely get something totally different: Ross trying to understand his gay wife's predilection, Rachel contemplating an affair with a married man, Monica trying to lose her virginity, with words like "bitch" and "bastard" sprinkled throughout conversations.

TV producers used to be more restricted to reflecting the lives and values of the majority of its viewers. But in a been-there, done-that mode, Hollywood today seems inclined to turn its back on traditional family themes, opting instead for the non-traditional take ("Party of Five," "Once and Again"). Or it uses the sitcom vehicle to explore alternative adult lifestyles ("Will and Grace"). Another trend has networks battling it out in the "confront and provoke" department ("Jerry Springer," "Divorce Court")—all in the name of entertaining daytime programming. We've come so far so fast: when the sitcom was in its infancy, Rob and Laura Petrie were forced to sleep in separate beds; now middle-aged, the sitcom has become more daring, offering its audiences such titillating scenes as same-sex kissing ("Ally McBeal").

That particular "Ally McBeal" episode was banned in Singapore, because it was created around "alternative sexual explorations," according to a small news item in *The National Post*. In contrast, when it aired in November 1999 in Canada and the U.S., it drew the show's largest audience ever. North Americans seem to be lapping up whatever's thrown their way, the proof is in the ratings. So where does TV go from here? One thing's certain, as the envelope on acceptable themes is pushed,

How Kids Spend Time

Watching TV:
64%

Reading for pleasure:
20%

Listening to CDs or tapes:
19%

Listening to the radio:
17%

Using a computer for fun:
9%

Playing video games:
8%

On-line:
3%

Playing computer games:
2%

Source: *Kids & Media @ The New Millennium*, Kaiser Family Foundation, Fall 1999.

today's kids will be continually exposed to new ideas and lifestyle alternatives. TV pushes them to think about situations and lifestyles and options ahead of when they would naturally, to grow up more quickly.

Always On, Always Available

Not only are there more TV choices, but more kids now have their own TVs. According to the KFF study, two-thirds of American kids over eight and one-third of kids aged two to seven have a TV in their bedroom. Two-thirds also claim to have the TV on during mealtimes while 60 per cent have no rules about TV at all.

We hear about the increase in computer and Internet access in North American homes, but obviously TV still rules with kids. According to the Kaiser study, while 64 per cent of kids watch TV for more than an hour a day, only about 9 per cent use the computer for fun.

Over time Internet activities may overtake, or at least catch up to, TV as the popular choice of entertainment, as a recent survey by Young Culture Inc., a Toronto-based research firm reported in spring 2000. Their phone survey of 1,000 teens showed that 85 per cent of teens spend just over nine hours on-line every week. This is about the same time they devote to watching TV.

But for the most part TV still rocks, especially among younger kids. It's the "command centre of the culture," says American critic and communications theorist Neil Postman, who has authored several books including *The Disappearance of Childhood* and *Amusing Ourselves to Death*. It's true, kids pick up a lot of audiovisual cues from the small screen. From what to wear to what music to listen to, TV usually has the answers kids want, to help them better define themselves. And parents, unwittingly, may be pushing their kids into watching new and different shows they don't approve of, in the millennial scenario of rebellious youth in search of identity.

Television plays a pivotal role in how kids define themselves.

"In some ways, it's probably harder for kids to find a way to express their separateness from adults these days," says parenting writer Holly Bennett, editorial director of Today's Parent Group in Toronto and co-author of a series of parenting books called *Steps and Stages*. "Consider the 10-year-old who adores 'The Simpsons' because of the show's 'authority sucks' attitude—until he finds himself laughing at the same jokes as his parents. Pretty deflating to a kid trying to be cool. As a result, these preteens might end up going a bit farther afield to find an aspect of popular culture that they can call their own—enter 'Beavis and Butthead'!"

For the kid trying to be cool, TV is an easy fit, says Alan Mirabelli, executive director of administration and communications at the Vanier Institute of the Family in Ottawa, a non-profit organization established in 1965 that focuses on family issues. If you've ever been one of those kids desperate to belong to a clique in that heartless arena known as the schoolyard, you can appreciate the value of TV more. "Television was once looked upon as education. Now kids also use the medium of TV to fit in. The one common thing kids in the schoolyard share is the show they watched the night before. It's a shared experience."

Another shared experience is that many young kids are watching prime-time programming meant for adults. "Kids as young as four watch shows such as 'The Simpsons' and 'South Park.' Younger children are watching material that's not designed for them," says Clive VanderBurgh, head of The School of Radio and Television Arts, Ryerson Polytechnic University in Toronto, who conducts annual research on kids and TV.

Many of the shows kids are watching today feature characters several years (even decades) older than them and these shows expose them to ideas and language they might not otherwise be privy to for several more years (see Figure 2).

Marrying Technologies: Internet on TV

Will the Internet/ computer eventually overtake TV, the way TV surpassed radio? Not likely, says Clive VanderBurgh, professor and head of television and video at the School of Radio and Television Arts, Ryerson Polytechnic University in Toronto. In fact, he forecasts something else entirely: convergence. "I believe that TV and the Internet/ computer will become one. You'll be able to watch TV in an interactive mode or the traditional passive mode. Traditional TV will be streamed online and you'll be able to access the Net on your TV. Either TV will take over the Internet with interactivity, or the Internet will take over TV, but they're going to converge."

FIGURE 2: *Top Shows for Kids and Adults*

Everyone's Watching the Same Shows		
Children 2–11	**Teens 12–17**	**Adults 25–54**
1. Pokemon	1. Simpsons	1. Frasier
2. Friends	2. That 70's Show	2. Friends
3. Digimon	3. Friends	3. X-Files
4. Arthur	4. X-Files	4. ER
5. Magic School Bus	5. Dharma & Greg	5. Ally McBeal
6. Pingu	6. Dawson's Creek	6. Stark Raving Mad
7. Simpsons	7. Millionaire	7. Jesse
8. Rug Rats	8. Jesse	8. Millionaire
9. Popular Mech. Kids	9. Get Real	9. Law & Order
10. Millionaire	10. Frasier	10. The Practice

Source: *Neilsen Media Research, Canada, Fall 1999.*

Why do kids watch more adult-programming now? It's simple, says Kealy Wilkinson, former national director of the Alliance for Children and Television (ACT). "In the old days, there were only four or five broadcast channels and part of their mandate was to broadcast appropriate programs at appropriate times. Now we have 60 channels, or more. Many don't have any responsibility to broadcast to children; they're specialty channels geared to adults." In addition, viewing habits have changed a lot. "Kids used to watch mainly in the morning and late afternoon. Now, it's primarily young kids watching after 4 p.m. Older kids are watching after supper and in the early evening because they're busy after school doing different activities."

The Vanier Institute's Mirabelli adds: "TV doesn't have the same barriers as the print medium. Kids can't be exposed to things beyond their maturity in print if they can't read them." When you add the lack of barriers to the fact that during the 1980s cable services allowed for an explosion of new channels and specialty services geared to adults, says Wilkinson, it's easy to understand how suddenly more kids could access more adult programming.

The Influence of TV Advertising

Of course, watching TV, adult-oriented or not, means being exposed to advertising, which also affects the way children think and act. It was this very thought that sent policy makers scurrying to develop advertising guidelines several decades ago. The interest in children as consumers of media and products goes back 30 years, says Donna Lero, co-director of the Centre for Families, Work and Well-Being at the University of Guelph. "In the 1970s and 1980s, there was real concern that TV ads didn't recognize that kids could not distinguish between programs and ads." Ultimately, this led to the Code of Ethics in Advertising, which subsequently has led to the acceptance and legitimacy of children as consumers. We now see increased brand consciousness of children in the 1990s," Lero says.

By the age of seven, TV watchers will have seen an average of at least 20,000 commercials a year, says Kealy Wilkinson, formerly of The Alliance for Children and Television. VanderBurgh says children are influenced by commercials, even if they don't understand them. In *There's Always the Fine Print*, a 1997–98 Canadian study co-produced by Ryerson University's departments of Radio and Television Arts and Early Childhood, Vander-Burgh's students interviewed over 2,000 kids over two years to better understand their viewing and purchasing habits.

They found that kids aged two to five had difficulty saying which products they bought because of a TV show or commercial, but the majority of items were dolls or action figures depicting characters on favourite TV shows. This age group doesn't really understand the message being broadcast in the commercials, he said, but, when they watch them repeatedly, they are influenced.

Child Development and TV

Age 2-5
- May know TV isn't real
- Pays a lot of attention to commericals
- Trusts commercials
- Doesn't know there is a difference between commercials and programs

Age 6-9
- Pays a lot of attention to commercials
- Can tell the difference between a commercial and a program

(Continued on next page)

Child Development and TV
(Continued from previous page)

- Begins to recognize that the purpose of a commercial is to persuade

Age 10-14
- Less interested in commercials
- Knows the difference between programs and commercials
- Knows that the intent of the commercial is to persuade and understands some persuasion techniques

Source: *Minding the Set*, a booklet published by The Alliance for Children and Television

These findings are in stark contrast to the next age group, the six- to nine-year-olds. A full 89 per cent of this group was able to name a product they bought because of a TV show or commercial. Additionally, half these kids could identify a commercial that didn't tell the truth about its products, though the younger portion (the six- and seven-year-olds) had more difficulty distinguishing between what was truthful and what was not.

In the 10 to 12 age group, 29 per cent of kids said they bought an item as a direct result of a TV show or commercial. As for the products most likely to show up on their list of untruthful commercials? Food items were number one.

The 13 to 15 age group was influenced by TV to buy more clothing than any other age range, with makeup and food trailing close behind. It is this group, says VanderBurgh, that is most likely to watch entertainment programs targeted for a general adult audience.

Computer Culture

Has anything transformed our lives more quickly and completely than computers? Cars? TVs? Phones? These are all revolutionary innovations that have unequivocally changed our lives. But as quickly and com-pletely as computers? No.

The computer culture has permeated every aspect of life, from how we work to how we play, in less than a generation. The transition for many adults has not been without frustration. But for today's teen, computers and other electronic gadgets are a life necessity, just helping them keep pace with the demands of society, says *American Demographic*. "Being a teenager today means you need a pager, an e-mail address (which means you need a computer, preferably your own), and maybe even a cellphone," a December 1999 article called "Play Dough" states.

To a lesser extent, this is also the reality for today's younger kids. Computers are as much a part of their life as the air they breath, and computer technology influences kids (and those around them) in ways previous generations could never have fathomed.

For the first time in human history, says Don Tapscott, chairman of the Alliance for Converging Technologies, and author of *Growing Up Digital: The Rise of the Net*, children are "knowledge authorities" in a crucial area—they are passing on cultural information and technological skills to their parents. While adults scramble to keep pace with this fast-moving technology, kids not only take it in their stride, they share their expertise. This is healthy, says Tapscott, because it creates more of a peer dynamic within families. "If managed well by parents, it can create a more open, consensual and effective family unit."

Some parents lament that computers are rushing kids through childhoods and putting undue pressure on them academically. Students in grades as junior as four and five are encouraged to submit computer-typed school projects with colour-printed title pages. Are computers enabling and illuminating our kids' lives, or are they darkening and disabling them?

Both may be true. No question, computers enhance our kids' learning capabilities. From CD-ROM games such as the Blaster series by Davidson (edutainment CDs aimed at kids as young as three, with titles like Math Blaster, Science Blaster, Reading Blaster), to the sweeping selection of information available for school projects on-line, nothing compares to the computer's capaciousness.

But consider this situation. As the time between project assignment and due date shrinks to accommodate tighter teaching schedules—the

Media Evolution

Interestingly, television's evolution is following in the footsteps of radio's. Consider this excerpt from a 1948 issue of *Parents* magazine: "Our family is rather close knit anyhow, yet with practically every room having a radio it was not uncommon for all to scatter to enjoy particular programs. With one television set our family is brought together as a unit for a while after dinner."

This same statement could be true today if we replace "radio" for "TV" and "TV" for "computer." One wonders how the generation 50 years hence will fill in the blanks?

reality of education in the 2000s—a new dilemma comes to light. For kids with computers, shorter work spans don't present much of a hardship—the bulk of information is only a couple of mouse clicks away. But what of the child without a computer? He's forced to rely on Mom or Dad to take him to the local library, or to wait for a response, via snail mail, from a corporation's PR department, before he can even begin composing his essay.

> The Internet has emboldened kids, making them more confident then ever before.

It's a concern many parents share. In a recent Media Awareness Network survey, *Canada's Children in a Wired World: The Parents' View*, which polled 1,080 Canadian families to determine parents' views about the Net, 80 per cent of parents say it is the way of the future and believe that if they are not on-line they will be left behind. Clearly, the computer that can so easily enable one child, can just as surely disable another.

Tapscott refers to this as the "digital divide." There is a direct correlation between income and access to computers. As society thrusts forward in its digital revolution, those without computers will be left in the technological vacuum of yesteryear. The larger sociological and economical implications are that we will move from a world of haves and have nots, to a world of cans and cannots. (See Figure 3 for the correlation of households with com-

FIGURE 3: *Highest Income Households Likely to Have Computer*

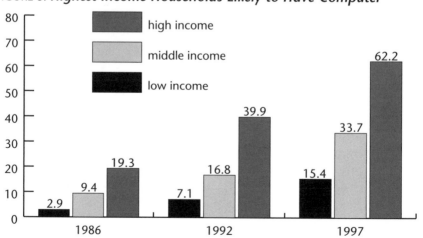

Source: *Figures from Statistics Canada. "Household Facilities and Equipment (HFE) Survey," in* The Daily, *March 20, 1998.*

puters and household incomes.) With the quickened pace of technological change, this becomes a very serious global problem, because it is difficult to catch up. Ideally, the more we understand and respect the power of the computer—and its spinoff, the Internet—the better prepared we will be to meet future challenges.

We can start by understanding what effect the Net has in our lives today. How is it contributing to the changing status of the child within our family model? This is a question adults grapple with because there are no "gut feelings." Without comparable childhood experiences to help them define this technological revolution, adults have no internal barometer to measure the influence of change.

We do know that this ever-expanding digital world coursing through our modem, literally brings the world to our children's doorstep. Curious about China? Looking for a French penpal? Need the names of the Renaissance artists? It's at your fingertips. But is this "instant information" helpful?

Yes, says Tapscott. This easy access to data does have a positive influence on kids, it emboldens them. Not only can they find the research they need for school projects, today's kids are going on-line to research major household items such as cars, home entertainment equipment, cameras, clothes and, of course, computers. "Corporations are falling over themselves to put easily retrieved information on the Web. If the info you want isn't posted, simply send an e-mail for further details. Many companies sponsor or tie-in to discussion rooms so that consumers can discuss their product and help each other make the best use of the good or service."

Protecting On-Line Privacy

To deal with the issues of privacy, The Children's Online Privacy Protection Act (COPPA) was launched in spring 2000. Its mandate is to protect children from manipulative and exploitive marketing and advertising Internet practices, says Kathryn Montgomery, Ph.D., president of the Center for Media Education (CME), a nonprofit organization set up to create a quality electronic media culture.

COPPA establishes a set of rules to help guide the development of this new marketplace. COPPA requires commercial Web sites targeted to kids under age 13 to:

- Provide clear notice of what personal information children are being asked for and how it is to be used.

(Continued on next page)

**Protecting
On-Line Privacy**
(Continued from previous page)

- Obtain verifiable
  parental consent
  (for example, a
  signed authoriza-
  tion form mailed
  or faxed back to
  the Web site;
  a call to a toll-
  free number by
  a parent) in
  most instances,
  before collecting
  and using a
  child's personal
  information.
- Provide parents
  access to the
  personal informa-
  tion collected from
  their child and the
  right to prevent
  further use.

For more information,
visit COPPA's Web site:
www.KidsPrivacy.org

This ability to participate in purchasing decisions boosts children's confidence and gives them a feeling of contributing to the family in new ways. It's a sensation never experienced by previous generations. Flash back 20 years and it's difficult to conjure up any comparable image of economic clout resting in the hands of children. One boomer recalls being summarily dismissed by a salesclerk when she went on her first solo shopping expedition. She was viewed as slightly suspicious, not a serious customer. The Net, however, is the great equalizer. Every surfer—ageless, faceless—is a potential customer. The trickle-down effect is that a kid who has gained confidence from navigating on-line is less likely to let himself be intimidated by a rude store clerk, or by anyone else for that matter.

"Today's kids are far less hesitant than any generation before them to express their views. Kids blast off e-mails to politicians, corporations, teachers and others as they do their on-line research," says Tapscott. "They ask questions without hesitation. They are confident that their views have merit, and do not unquestioningly accept whatever they are told. "

In Canada, Internet use is high in families with a computer, according to the Media Awareness Network survey, conducted by the Toronto-based Environics Research Group. Over 70 per cent of parents with children between six and 16 who have a computer indicate they have Internet access at home, and 86 per cent of these say their children use the Internet.

And what of the less attractive side of the Net? In a world without borders, kids are bound to end up in places they don't belong—adult chat rooms and pornography sites, for example. According to the survey, 61 per cent of parents think their children would know what to do if they found themselves in an uncomfortable situation; 39 per cent are not so sure.

As in all areas of parenting, families need to keep balance in mind as they plough down the information highway. Otherwise, it's easy to let technology have undue influence.

Steve Bennett, who has written more than 55 books on computing, parenting, the environment and business, offers some solid advice in his latest book, *The Plugged-in Parent: What You Should Know About Kids and Computers.* He suggests families can find a satisfactory balance between the wired and real worlds by keeping the computer in its place. "So much depends on how we present the computer to our kids—whether we put it on a pedestal or introduce it as a powerful, yet pedestrian, appliance. In households that take the appliance approach, the computer becomes just another tool."

Parents delight at the self-assurance and poise their children glean from their technological prowess, and adults should welcome the opportunity to share these new experiences. But there's another aspect of the Net we must be wary of, says Alan Mirabelli of the Vanier Institute in Ottawa. It's easy to get caught up in the boon of technology, to feel pressured to go faster and faster, but it's important to remember that homes need to be a retreat: the place people go to close the door on the automated world, and to revel in being a family.

Web Statistics

- 55% of parents think their children always ask permission before submitting information to Web sites
- 46% think their children have learned to protect their privacy; 50% are not so sure
- 44% think their children have learned to judge if on-line information is reliable and truthful; 52% are not so sure
- 21% of children have come across sexually explicit material on the Net
- 6% of children have been sent unsolicited sexual material
- 4% of children have met someone in person whom they first met on the Internet

Source: *Canada's Children in a Wired World*, Media Awareness Network.

SPEED READ SUMMARY

TVs and PCs have the capacity to empower, embolden and elevate kids.
But with opportunity comes some risk, which parents need to balance
as their children enter brave new worlds:

- StatsCan says kids aged two to 11 watch an average of 17.9 hours of TV a week (2.56 hours a day)
- Teens aged 12 to 17 watch an average of 16.9 hours weekly (2.41 hours a day)
- TV is the "command centre" of kid culture—influencing kids' choices of what to wear, what music to listen to
- More channels means more kids watch adult-themed TV
- Inconsistency in TV story lines makes it hard to find appropriate family viewing
- Over 70 per cent of parents with kids between six and 16 have Internet access at home; 86 per cent say their children use the Internet
- Children are "knowledge authorities" on the Net, passing on cultural information and technological skills to parents
- The Net is a great equalizer—every surfer is ageless and faceless. This, along with its instant access, emboldens kids

5

Influence in Action

Youth is the best time to be rich,
and the best time to be poor.
—*Euripides*

CD players, TVs with satellite dishes, VCRs, DVDs, computers with Internet access, cellphones, pagers, and video game sets in pocket- or regular-sized versions—technology rules. The full impact of such a major force will be years in assessing. But there are a few things we know for certain already. Technology facilitates the evolution of youth culture, elevating today's kids to unprecedented heights. The other influences on the adultification of kids—changing family attitudes, sports, multiculturalism and travel— all have an impact, but without the aid of technology they are self-limiting. Technology changes how children think about the world and how they react to it. In this chapter we look at how technology has contributed to kids' savvy through the development of their pop culture, how it has fuelled the desire for "more," and how, ultimately, it has changed their expectations of the world around them.

Kids' Pop Culture

Some media critics are wary of what is happening in the child-entertainment industry, pointing fingers at what they call thinly veiled attempts to disguise entertainment as sales pitches devoid of morals.

In a June 30, 1997 issue of *Business Week*, "Hey Kids, Buy This!" by David Leonhardt and Kathleen Kerwin, it was reported that: "Instead of transmitting a sense of who we are and what we hold important, today's marketing-driven culture is instilling in [children] the sense that little exists without a sales pitch attached and that self-worth is something you buy at a shopping mall."

Canadian media critic Kathleen McDonnell, author of *Kid Culture* and the just released *Childhood Without Walls: Growing Up in the Multimedia Age*, has been observing kids and kid culture for many years. While she does believe there is truth to the sales pitch idea, she doesn't buy into any Chicken Little angst. "It's not helpful to throw up our hands and write off multimedia. To me, it brings home the idea that future generations will be growing up in a different media universe and we're still not used to this one."

There are still CDs, videos, books, movies and TV that are written or created for the sole purpose of entertaining and teaching children. There is a wonderful array of literature that captures the imagination of kids— witness the best-selling Harry Potter series by J. K. Rowling. Other contemporary children's authors include Robert Munsch, Marc Brown (*Arthur*) and Paulette Bourgeois (*Franklin*). Movie producers are still interested in bringing classics to the silver screen: E. B. White's *Stuart Little* is one such offering. And we don't have to look further than *Thomas and the Magic Railroad* to find redemptive qualities in film; devoid of violence or foul language, the movie teaches children the importance of loyalty and the benefits of teamwork. The small screen also offers a strong variety of educational and entertaining shows for children such as "Blue's Clues," "Rugrats," "Big Comfy Couch" or "Teletubbies." As for CDs for kids, they have introduced a whole new area of entertainment— wonderful opportunities for kids to play and learn at once. Microsoft Home's *The Magic School Bus* and Edumark's *Sammy's Science House* and *Imagination Express* are just a few examples. Most of these current pop culture examples do indeed come with their own marketing initiative— or will soon—to sell plush toys, games and other kiddie delights. But to say they are nothing more than a sales pitch without moral value would be unfairly dismissive.

A truer end result of our marketing-driven culture may be this: kids' expectations of their world have grown. Thirty years ago, only a handful of TV shows existed for the benefit of kids: "The Mickey Mouse

Show," "Mr. Dressup," "The Friendly Giant," and "Romper Room," for instance. Contrast that with today's picks, which gives kids a wide variety of shows and around-the-clock programming. The developing pop culture has allowed kids from the outset to think in terms of choice, and so they continue to expect more.

And the world delivers. Television is not the only medium to provide vast selection. Take magazines. Until recently there were a handful for kids, and mostly for older ones—think *Highlights*, *Young Miss*, *Tiger Beat*, and *Mad Magazine*. Today, kids have their own section in bookstores. There is a magazine for virtually every subject of interest to the younger set: animals, video games, crafts, travel, dolls and even junior versions of well-known grown-up publications: *Sports Illustrated for Kids*, *Cosmo Girl*, and *Teen People* are but a few examples.

All this choice adds up to a generation of media-conscious kids. Instead of transmitting the idea that self-worth is something kids buy at the mall, our marketing-driven culture and multimedia world mean that kids learn early on how to interpret and react to a society that is falling over itself to cater to them. The best example of this comes through when you look at fads and trends among kids. Says Kathleen McDonnell, "I don't really believe that kids' phenomena are due to sales and marketing. Phenomena usually build in kids' networks … Pokémon travelled by kids' word of mouth," she says.

Kids may not be immune to marketing, but they are discerning. Having so much choice has contributed to this. "Kids are intelligent. When they do fall for marketing, it's because there's something behind it. It's not because they're brainwashed or mindlessly consuming it because they're told to consume it," says McDonnell.

Fashion and Music Rule on Web

The Top 10 sites for Generation Y at home were:

Ae.com (American Eagle clothing)

Ohhla.com (lyrics)

Nsyncdirect.com (musical group)

delias.com

Seventeen.com (magazine)

Teen.com (teen portal)

Sparknotes.com (study notes)

Abercrombie.com (clothing)

Lyrics.astraweb.com (lyrics)

Blink182.com (musical group)

Source: Neilsen Net Ratings reported in *Advertising Age* in April 2000.

Scott Hawkins, who teaches the marketers of tomorrow in his role as associate professor at the Rotman School of Management, University of Toronto, agrees. "Younger people are exposed to so much more and they're rather cynical about the intentions and objectives of marketers. They attribute or look for negative connotations in marketing."

Kids now have a chance to develop critical thinking skills that previous generations never had. They are neither gullible nor naïve. Says McDonnell: "Kids are very caught up in marketing, but are very critical also. They are so hyperaware of labels and brand names. They're very ready to talk about whether something measures up to its advertiser's claims. They're very ready to talk about when they think ads are phony or trying to manipulate them. Kids my daughter's age (11) are media savvy and much more critical of their environment."

Hawkins adds that today's young audiences are sophisticated and better able to filter information. "After they're seven or eight, they understand the difference between a commercial and program and will very quickly get into filtering mode when exposed to the influence of the media, like television."

Evidence of this exists in the type of advertisements that were popular decades ago, that now don't see the light of day. "Twenty years ago, advertisers took a more slice-of-life/hidden-camera approach with ads. They'd show a woman doing her laundry and talking about a product with friends and the situation would be meant to look real. Today's consumer is more aware those ads are just a set-up."

Prosperity

Kids are born expecting extras and conveniences, it's part and parcel of life in the multimedia age. Technology is also greatly responsible for fuelling the desire for "more."

> **Our technological world has fostered kids' expectation for convenience and extras.**

Unlike adults, who have retrofitted their lives around the many and varied advances of technology, kids have never known a different lifestyle. CD players can be programmed to play for hours on end, phones have built-in display screens to say who's calling and give the option of answering or not, TVs turn on and off with wireless remotes or by preset buttons.

Today's kids cannot fathom life without digital technology and the many conveniences it has provided. They are entranced with electronic gadgets and play around with the different buttons and options, whereas many adults are still afraid, a little in awe, of them. While being able to tape a TV program or pause a show midway through to take a snack break are still little miracles to those over 35, to kids they're just an average life skill. The pace of technology adoption in the last decade has brought more technology into our lives, faster. Learning to master new skills has always been an important step in child development and in today's world that includes mastering technology at a very young age.

The Acceleration of "More"

Add a consuming culture to the mix, and change really begins to brew. In the 1970s most neighbourhood kids were in a similar economic situation. Like today's young people, they knew what was cool thanks to their ever-expanding access to the world stage, but there was one distinguishing feature between then and now. In the '70s, kids seldom asked for stuff and if they did, parents rarely acquiesced. Sure, kids had wish lists back then too. But wants didn't always translate into successful shopping trips. Shopping was a rare excursion in many households. It was not a pleasurable pastime—but a practical pursuit. And when boomer kids asked their parents to buy something at the store, the standard comeback was: "We don't have money for extras like that."

Today the extras have become "mandatories." We have evolved from an "I want" world to an "I need" world. Parents constantly hear, "Mom, I really *need* to have that Gap vest." Of course, the vest is not a necessity. It's not a life need, but a life want.

Add to that a culture fattened off the consuming habits of its self-indulged boomer generation, and you have a society that really doesn't know how to say no to its children. The cycle of consumption grows when you factor in that a two-income household can provide for more, and that smaller families can make money go further. The cycle is fed by the fact that some working parents indulge their kids out of guilt or desire for the kids to have what they were denied in youth. So strong is the hunger to provide more that experts tell us there is evidence kids in homes without the means for extra still get it. Says Clair Hawes, a

Vancouver psychologist whose clinic services families across the socioe-
conomic board, "It amazes me that people with very little money can
garner resources to buy their kids things. They seem so concerned that
kids are going to miss out on something that they're trying to fill in all
the gaps. The base level of stuff kids have is much higher than parents
can afford *or* kids need." Pat McGill, a teacher in Ottawa and father of
two children agrees. He sees kids in his school packing cellphones,
pagers and all the latest electronic gear. "The kids from my school come
from homes of cabinet makers and cabinet ministers and regardless
they have it all."

The idea of "more" is both tantalizing and tangible especially in our
digital age: few things rival technology's ability to facilitate "more."
Video games clearly illustrate this intoxicating desire. To a child, a
video game represents a challenge to master new moves and win.
Successive levels fuel the competitive drive until the child finally
conquers the game in its entirety. The cycle repeats itself with each new
game purchased. Before you know it, the child has accumulated an
entire shelf of electronic victories and is turning to his mom with the
familiar refrain: "I've got nothing to play."

In the world of technology, this cycle never ends. You only need
look at what's gathering dust in the basements of today's teenagers to
see how well the "more" culture in video game technology is thriving.
Remember Pong? It's ancient when compared with the newest interpretation of games that have three-dimensional visuals and sponta-
neous commentary. Consider that Nintendo launched its new format
in 1988 and since then we have seen three different platforms developed (NES [Nintendo Entertainment System], Super NES and Nintendo
64), each with more sophisticated graphics and improved video and
player interaction. One household with children under 18 could very
easily have faced the kid demand to have four systems.

**Kids know
that more is
coming and act
accordingly.**

The latest generation is programmed to know
that there will always be "a next best thing" often
before they have outgrown or finished with the last
thing. Kids have learned this from the adults
around them who lease cars for two-year periods,
add to their CD collection on a whim, buy new
kitchen appliances simply for a change.

Allison Liss, the owner of Lunatic Fringe, a teen fashion store in Toronto, believes everything is faster now. "When I was a kid, if you had a pair of pants, you wore them 'til you grew out of them or wore them out. Now shopping is recreation and we are more wasteful." One boomer's experience illustrates this point: "my husband complained to me that he needed a new coat. When I questioned him about the need when he had a fairly new coat already in the closet he answered, 'but the buttons have fallen off that one.'"

And while some argue that the pendulum is swinging back towards moderation, it may be too late for Generation Y whose need for more is ingrained in their psyche. Douglas Rushkoff says today's youth—whom he refers to as "screenagers" (think TV, films and computers)—are educated in speed. According to Rushkoff, being able to cope with speed is going to be a necessity of the 21st century. In his book *Playing the Future: What We Can Learn From Digital Kids*, Rushkoff says the intensity of evolutionary change shows no signs of slowing down and that all of us need to adapt to that fact. The workplace of the future will require broader attention ranges and shorter absorption times so that we can process visual information more rapidly. "This information skimming will need to be practiced on many different levels, and sometimes simultaneously."

Today's "more" approach to consumerism is in drastic opposition to the pre-war value of "less."

The result is a 180-degree turn in thinking from a century ago: Rushkoff's futuristic model based on "more" is the exact opposite of the pre-war generation's steadfast belief in "less." Our principles of consumption have changed dramatically. Depression-era parents believed consumption ethics were about saving and sacrifice. To waste meant you didn't care about the future of your family, your neighbourhood or your country. Lack of consumption was linked to civic duty.

Today, we travel a different path. The edict "use it up, wear it out, make do or do without" is more in keeping with our 3Rs philosophy of dealing with garbage issues, not consumer goods. A generation that has been preoccupied with consuming, that has only known economic prosperity, cannot understand the sacrifices other generations have lived with. The boomer generation grew up in a time of expansion and

That's Garbage!

Waste not, want not—it's a phrase that doesn't exactly roll off the tongue of today's older boomer. The generation that grew up in prosperity doesn't have the built-in values of the Depression/pre-war generations, says Becky Graninger of the U.S. firm Wise Recycling. Instead of making do or reusing, Graninger says older boomers buy more things and throw more things away. The end result? Fewer people are recycling today. According to the Aluminum Association, the number of cans collected for recycling was down for 1998, a trend the association is expecting will continue when 1999's numbers are tabulated.

opportunity. They are the optimists who believe in ever-expanding possibilities and they have passed on those beliefs to their offspring. Boomers don't save, they spend. They don't sacrifice things, they experience things. The *Journal of Consumer Research* recently reported that a mere 10 to 15 per cent of the population today practises frugality. For the most part we are living in the lap of materialism. And while the boomers' belief that the "good times were for all times" was temporarily shaken with the Big Crash of '89, the economy in the last 10 years has proven that was an aberration and not an end to life as they knew it.

As for the "don't waste" mentality they heard as kids, they've totally rejected it. Remember the conspicuous consumption of the 1980s? The boomers were labelled greedy, self-important and materialistic by an older generation of media people who could not understand how they could be so loose with their money. This attitude toward money, spending and experiencing has greatly impacted the boomers' children. Consumer behaviour experts say that the consumer is not born but produced by a process that encourages them to want and want. Some theorists have called this a "culture-ideology of consumerism." Essays from the book *The Cultures of Globalization* discuss how this culture "persuades people to consume above their biological needs in order to perpetuate the accumulation of capital for private profit." In one essay titled "Social Movements and Capitalism" the author Leslie Sklair says the culture ideology of consumerism asserts that the meaning of life is to be found in the things we possess: "To consume is to be fully alive and to remain alive we must continually consume."

It is evident to most of us that we live in a consumer world because our behaviour reminds us of it weekly. Stores and the mall have become a place where we spend a lot of time. Shopping is the second-most important leisure-time activity in the United States (behind television viewing, which likely promotes shopping). Where Americans on average spent 20 minutes on a trip to the mall in the 1960s, in the 1990s that rose to an average of 3 hours or more. The mall has become a public space which encourages buying, eating, and viewing entertainment. All consuming activities—all which feed the need for more.

If the boomers were the "me" generation, then Generation Y could be thought of as the "more" generation. As one *New Yorker* cartoon glibly pointed out, these kids have only known a "bull market." The end result: More spending, more experiencing, more demands for more.

"Of course he looks peaceful—he's lived his entire life in a bull market."

SPEED READ SUMMARY

- Technology facilitates the evolution of kid culture, changing how kids think about the world and how they react to it.
- A burgeoning pop culture has taught kids to expect more in terms of choice and control.
- Technology creates an insatiable appetite for more. Video games, for instance, are built with more in mind; players can't win until they do more—master new moves and levels that eventually let them conquer the game.

- The appetite spreads to other areas of consumption. The "extras" that boomers' parents occasionally bestowed on kids become "mandatories" for Generation Y. They expect extras and conveniences.
- Boomers and their progeny reject the "don't waste" mentality of their own parents. They don't save, they spend; they don't sacrifice, they indulge. If the boomers were the "me" generation, this latest generation could be thought of as the "more" generation.

6

Why Kids Mean Business

A billion here, a billion there.
Pretty soon it adds up to real money.
—Senator Everett Dirksen and Josh on "The West Wing"

The idea that Generation Y is the "more" generation fits well with the financial picture painted by economists. *Kids buy a lot.* There are estimates that kid spending has doubled during each decade of the 1960s, 1970s and 1980s and has tripled in the 1990s. Numbers are being reported in every article and book written about kids. Huge numbers. Not surprisingly there is little consistency to the numbers reported from different sources but the sources all agree on one thing—the dollar figures are in the billions and they are going up.

To shed some light on the magnitude of the economic powerhouse that kids represent, Figure 1 outlines the range that has been reported in books and major publications in the late 1990's:

FIGURE 1 *Media Reported Spending by North American Kids*

U.S. kids aged 4–12 in 1997 spent from	$11 billion to 24.4 billion
U.S. teens aged 13–19 in 1998 spent from	$94 billion to $121 billion
Canadian tweens aged 9–14 in 1999 spent	$ 1.6 billion
Canadian youth aged 12–24 spent	$13.5 billion

Sources: *U.S.: NPD Group; Canadian:* YTV Kid and Tween Report, *1999, Canadian Broadcast Sales Report on kids' spending in 1998/99*

So What Does It All Add Up To?

In today's marketplace kids, tweens, and teens mean business. A lot of business. If we take the conservative estimate the *U.S. market alone* is experiencing the combined power of $105 billion in kids' pocket money. The United States is about 10 times the size of Canada so we have used the 10x rule to rough out a Canadian equivalent because the exact breakdown in ages is not available. If these numbers are accurate the Canadian kid market would be worth approximately $10.5 billion dollars.

Our calculation:

	Canadian Estimate	US Conservative Estimate
Kids 4–12	$ 1.1 billion	$ 11 billion
Teens 13–19	$ 9.4 billion	$ 94 billion
	$10.5 billion	$105 billion

Kids' spending in North America is over $115 billion each year.

If we look at a North American tally the market would be worth approximately $115 billion dollars.

The dollars being totalled are kids' discretionary money—their personal spending power. This does not include what their families spend, just what the individual kids are purchasing for their own pleasure. Over $100 billion is a lot of money and the numbers are going up. The U.S. estimates have kid and teen spending growing at $10 billion dollars a year and research from YTV (the kid TV channel) shows a steady increase in growth with Canadian tween spending increasing $100 million each year over the past four years.

If Not Trees, Where Does the Money Come From?

Kids want their own money. And they have it. But where do they get this money? When we talk to kids about this they mostly answer, "If I need it I ask for it." There are many U.S. sources on kids and their money. Books including *Kids as Customers* by Professor James McNeal, and *Wise Up to Teens*, share quantitative research showing how much kids spend and where they get the money. There is also a Canadian source for this information. YTV, the kid TV channel, has been tracking the spending habits of Canadian tweens aged nine to 14, since 1995. In 1999 YTV increased their study to include younger kids aged six to eight. They survey over 600 kids aged 6–14 every year, reporting their findings and figures from a 45-minute interview. This survey covers male and female kids and their parents, from families in all income brackets, in medium and large communities, in every province. *The YTV Kid & Tween Report* gives us an up-close look at Canadian kids, their money and their spending habits. In the next chapter we will review the Canadian information and comment on the comparisons to available U.S. data.

Kids and Their Money

Kids get money from a variety of sources including parents, relatives and jobs, but almost half of all tweens surveyed do receive an allowance which averages around seven dollars a week. But beyond allowances kids also get money at certain times of the year. Eighty-eight per cent of tweens said they receive money for their birthday. And back-to-school is one time of the year that stands out as an additional source of income for tweens, 34 per cent of tweens get extra shopping money at that time.

YTV has calculated that the Canadian tween market has $1.8 billion in 2000 to spend every year. Figure 2 illustrates how YTV arrives at that figure. Where do these $1.6 billion come from? Mostly parents shelling out. Even though it is considered "kids' money," the source is a parent's discretionary income. Fifty-four per cent of Canadian tweens have a regular allowance.

Kids getting allowance is not news. When boomers were growing up an allowance covered some penny candy at the corner store or, if saved, it helped toward a special purchase sometime during the year. Today tweens may get upwards of $10 dollars a week and teens can get

FIGURE 2 *Calculation of Canadian Tween Discretionary Income—1999*

Sources of Spending Money	Percent Who Receive	Number Who Receive	Dollar Amount	Factor	Annual Total
Weekly allowance	46.4	1,133,552	$7.80	52	$459,768,691
Back-to-school	34.2	835,506	$157.00	1	$131,174,442
Last birthday	88.1	2,152,000	$78.00	1	$167,856,000
Major holiday	62.3	1,521,989	$73.00	1	$111,105,197
Part-time job— hourly wage	13.1	320,033	$5.00 x 6.4 hrs.	52	$532,534,912
Part-time job— set price	8.5	207,655	$15.30 x week	52	$165,210,318
GRAND TOTAL					$1,567,649,560

Source: YTV Kid & Tween Report, *1999*.

four times that. So allowance can be lucrative, but it is the money beyond the allowance that really adds up. Allowances only account for one-third of a tween's income, according to *The YTV Kid & Tween Report*. Tweens received on average $7.80 a week and kids six to eight, $3.90 (See Figure 3). In the U.S., seven in 10 kids get an allowance of $6.00 to $8.00, and James McNeal of Texas A&M University, and the author of *Kids as Consumers*, claims it accounts for 45 per cent of their income.

FIGURE 3: *Kids' 6–8 Spending Money*

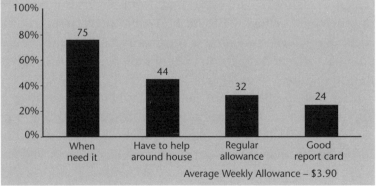

Source: YTV Kid & Tween Report, *1999*.

It is interesting to see the differences in sources of money in the different regions of Canada. Only 8 per cent of kids in French-speaking Quebec claim to get a regular allowance but a higher percentage of them get money for chores. In Quebec it's called "argent de poche" or pocket money. And parents in Quebec are surprised when told Quebec kids claim not to get allowance as often as other kids in Canada. One Francophone says: "Kids have a lot of money and it's not because they work. I see a lot of my kids' friends have money from their parents. They may not call it allowance but when they ask they get it."

FIGURE 4 *Tweens Spending Money Source*

English		French
90%	Last birthday	78%
77%	As needed	62%
65%	Major holiday	44%
54%	Per chore	86%
52%	Regular allowance	8%
39%	Back-to-school	4%
24%	Paying job	4%

Source: YTV Kid & Tween Report, *1999*.

Other parents in Quebec shared that there is no one way of giving money to the kids. Money can be handled as a standard allowance, given out based on chores, given as needed or deposited into bank accounts. One way or another kids in Quebec get the money they want.

As kids age, their spending needs increase and their sources of income change. While allowances continue to play a role it is a smaller one, compared to getting money as needed or from jobs in or out of the home. Kids and tweens do odd jobs like shovelling snow and yardwork and some tweens begin to make real money when they babysit. In 1999, 43 per cent of tweens made money babysitting, which has decreased since 1997 when 54 per cent of tweens babysat. When tweens do work for an hourly wage they are paid $5 an hour. Teens do the same types of jobs as tweens as well as take on part-time jobs at fast food restaurants or the local mall. However, employment income is not the driver in the recent increase in kid spending. The youth labour market is actually at its lowest point in 25 years, according to the Canadian Council on Social

Development. In 1989 two-thirds of 15- to 19-year-olds worked, and in 1997 it was less than half. The YTV poll shows the number of hours worked a week declining as well. In 1995 kids worked on average 7.3 hours a week whereas in 1999 they worked 6.4 hours a week. Some believe that this statistic is a result of increasing parental generosity, and a Rand Youth Poll found that affluent parents don' t want their children to work. "I want my kids to focus on school and their sports interests. They will be working the rest of their lives so I don't want to encourage them to work now. Especially when we can afford to give them some of the extra things they need," explains one parent who seems to speak for many today.

Beyond Allowances and Jobs

One of the most lucrative sources of income is the birthday present. Most tweens claimed that they receive about $60 on their special day. Add this to their weekly allowances ($7 x 4 weeks = $28) and kids have greater resources to buy their favourite things, especially in birthday month.

The money available to tweens doesn't stop at birthdays or allowances. As we discussed earlier, today's grandparents are younger (on average 59) and living longer. That means that in addition to kids getting money from Mom and Dad, they are also getting money from grandparents. David Foot calls these lucky kids the six-pocket children. "Because we have one-and-a-half kids today and we are living longer, kids have both sets of grandparents alive and their parents (= six adults with money in their pockets). Six-pocket kids are a reflection of the fact that we don't have as many kids to spread the money around." Referring once again to the U.S. research done by James McNeal, he states gift money from grandparents represents 10 per cent of kids' income now, rising from 5 per cent a decade ago. A Roper Starch report (a major U.S. research company who quantitatively tracks attitudes and behaviours) cited in *American Demographics* that grandparents estimate they spent a median of $400 per year on their grandchildren. In smaller households this could mean $100 or more per child a year. In Canada, *Today's Grandparent* magazine did a study that showed almost 40 per cent of those grandparents surveyed annually spend more than $100 on entertainment with their grandchildren and over 55 per cent spend more than $100 on clothing. These grandparents also invested for their loved ones. Twenty-one per cent opened a bank account and 18 per cent bought a Canada Savings Bond. With grandparents living longer, grandchildren can look forward to many years of their generosity.

Money is also given to kids at certain times of the year to manage extra purchases. The biggest bonanza is the perennial ritual of back-to-school. There is a good reason for the spike in retail sales in August and September as every family of school-aged kids doles out money to get their children outfitted for school. The money allocated to back-to-school has dramatically increased in the last two years according to the 1999 YTV study. Figure 5 shows that the average tween has $137 to spend on school supplies and clothes, which increased from $96 in 1996.

FIGURE 5: *Average Amount Tweens Have for Back-to-School Spending*

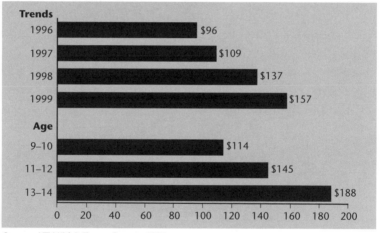

Source: YTV Kid & Tween Report, *1999*

So kids get their billions from a variety of structured sources like allowance, gifts, seasonal shopping and jobs, but they also get money on a more casual basis just by asking for it. A study by Merrill Lynch in the United States showed that 86 per cent of kids get money when they ask for it. Irma Zandl, of the Zandl Group, which specializes in trend research with the under-30 consumer, was quoted in *American Demographics* magazine: "A lot of parents are feeling guilty. They are working, their kids are coming home to empty houses so they want to make up for it." Zandl then says that boomers display a strong desire to be a friend to their child, rather than an authority figure, so kids often get what they want. Michael Adams author of *Sex in the Snow*, a study of the attitudes and values of Canadian adults, echoed these statements at a research conference. He referred to boomers as needing to connect with their kids as friends, evidenced by the affectionate terms they use such as "buddy and pal" when talking with their kids.

The need to be friends, or feelings of quilt, don't motivate all parents. Some, remembering the feelings of deprivation they experienced growing up in a middle-class environment where frugality was practiced, simply want to indulge their kids to make up for their own childhoods. And, finally, there are the parents who give just for the enjoyment of the act.

What Does $115 Billion Buy?

Candy and food rule when it comes to kids spending their own money. From youngest to oldest, candy is the number-one item bought. But while candy and other food top the lists, the total list is longer than one might expect and includes books, games and toys, music and clothing. One kid source claims that in the 1960s most of a kid's money would have been spent on candy, but now candy and drinks only represents one-third of their buying.

FIGURE 6 *What Kids and Tweens Buy*

Kids		Tweens
9%	Clothes/shoes	45%
49%	Candy	42%
11%	Food/drinks	22%
39%	Games/toys (not electronic)	21%
9%	Books/magazines	19%
4%	Music (e.g., CDs/tapes)	19%
6%	Video games	13%
7%	Pop	10%
13%	Ice cream	7%
10%	Gum	17%

Source: YTV Kid & Tween Report, *1999.*

Figure 6 shows that tweens spend their money on a wide variety of merchandise including things to eat, clothing, games, books and music. But if you are in the kid business you need to look at the differences between boys and girls because the reported *averages* are misleading. Figure 7 shows

How kids spend their money is very much gender specific.

that the majority of boys (44 per cent) claim to spend their money on candy, followed by non-electronic toys and games and clothing. The majority of girls (64 per cent) however, spend their money on clothes, followed by candy and food and drinks.

FIGURE 7 *Boys and Girls Buy Different Things*

BOYS		GIRLS	
Candy	44%	Clothes/shoes	64%
Games/toys (not electric)	27%	Candy	41%
Clothes/shoes	27%	Food/drinks	20%
Video games	25%	Books/magazines	19%
Food/drinks	24%	Music (e.g., CDs/tapes)	19%
Books/magazines	20%	Makeup	17%
Music (e.g., CDs/tapes)	19%	Games/toys (not electric)	15%

Source: YTV Kid & Tween Report, *1999*.

Older Kids Have More Cash

A major U.S. study of teens called the Teenage Marketing & Lifestyle study claims teens spend anywhere from $53 a week up to $125. This is serious money. At this stage the primary market is moving beyond penny candy and into higher ticket items. Teens buy more of everything. And while candy buying still remains high, the purchasing emphasis with teens now shifts to music and fast food for boys and movies and makeup for girls.

Because age changes the types of items that are bought, age also changes where the money is spent. Where you buy candy when you are seven is different from where you buy music when you are 13. So where do the kids spend their money?

Kids at different stages do have preferences on where to shop and they develop as consumers in a similar way, as their first store exposure is most likely that of a grocery store, according to research from Professor James McNeal. In the book *Kids as Customers*, McNeal examined the stages of shopping experiences and preferences. His research showed that kids graduate through the shopping world from the grocery store to the discount store to the specialty store. Forty-three per cent of children make their first independent purchase at a discount store, and 20 per cent at the grocery store. However, the first purchase doesn't make the discount store the dominant destination. Convenience stores get half of all kid purchases. Because these stores are on every corner in every neighbourhood they are accessible to all children, and they're full of merchandise young kids especially like: candy, chips, pop, trading cards.

FIGURE 8 *Stores Kids Prefer*

Young	Middle	Tween
convenience	mass discounter	mass discounter
supermarket	supermarket	specialty store
mass discounter	specialty store	supermarket

Source: *James McNeal, The Kids Market, 1999.*

As the kids grow, their shopping preferences change to include the broader range of merchandise they are interested in: clothing, toys, music, electronics. At this stage kids now find their needs met at the mall. The typical 10-year-old goes shopping with a parent two or three times a week, so he or she has access to a wide variety of store formats and can develop preferences of where to shop. Most kids can state a preference for a grocery store and they usually recommend it to their parents. Sixty-five per cent of kids visit a grocery store at least once a week. The same research shows that kids don't like drug stores or department stores, as they are seen as boring, too adult-like. At a conference in Arizona on marketing to kids and tweens, a presenter said that her research showed that tweens' favourite place to shop was at mass merchandisers and specialty stores. Tweens prefer mass merchandisers because they have the stuff that they like and it is priced affordably. They shop for clothes, personal care products, music, even room furnishings. Not surprisingly, mass merchandisers have been the fastest-growing retail sector in North America in the last few years. Specialty stores offer tweens distinct fashion looks and coveted brand names. As tweens' need to fit in increases, their need to have the right brands does as well. Both mass merchandisers and specialty stores at the mall are the destinations of choice to get the brands they desire.

SPEED READ SUMMARY

- North American Kids have over 115 billion U.S. dollars to spend each year. Kids get their money from their parents and other relatives through allowances, birthday gifts, back-to-school shopping, working and chores, and just when they ask for it.
- Younger kids, aged six to nine, get an average allowance of $3.90 a week
- Tweens get an average allowance of $7.80 a week
- Teens' weekly allowance can be $40 and up
- The money allocated to back-to-school purchases is increasing with the average tween in 1999 receiving $157 Canadian to spend on clothes and supplies
- Kids buy candy and tweens favour clothes as the first choice for spending their money
- Boys and girls have different preferences for how to spend their money. Boys like candy, toys, and clothes and video games, while girls prefer clothes, candy, food and magazines
- As kids grow older their interest in stores change. Kids start out preferring convenience and grocery stores and graduate to mass merchants and specialty stores

7

More Than Toys: An Overview of Kids' Economic Impact

$115 billion is just the tip of the iceberg of kids' economic clout. Kids get their own money and spend it, but beyond that they influence their family's purchases and are important for the purchasing power they will have as adults later in life. To help us understand the total impact of kidfluence the kid market has been studied and quantitifed by James McNeal, a professor of marketing at Texas A&M University. He has studied the consumer behaviour of children for over 25 years and is the author of many papers and books on the subject, the latest called *The Kids Market*.

Professor McNeal's studies have quantified the spending and shopping habits of kids, including their influence in the family, and through his published works he is considered the expert in this field. McNeal sets out three market segments to describe the economic impact kids have on the economy: he calls them the *primary* market, the *influence* market and the *future* market.

The primary market is the power of kids spending their own money on stuff for themselves like toys, clothes, candy, fast food and music. The primary market is the $115 billion we detailed in the previous chapter.

The influence market is where kids make an impact on adult purchases by either asking for something or getting a vote. Boomer parents have made a point of including their children in family decision-making and giving them a voice, as we noted earlier. Influences are apparent when Susan wants pizza for supper and Joshua wants his parents to take the family to the local theme park. It is also in action when a child helps decide on the home computer or family car purchase. This phenomenon is less understood but is growing in importance

It is estimated the kids' influence market is worth hundreds of billions.

because the family purchases create a much larger "kid" market for businesses to consider. James McNeal pegs the size of this market at $131 billion U.S. at a minimum. David Walsh, Ph.D, author of *Designer Kids*, and President of the National Institute on Media and Family in the United States, agrees with the power of the kidfluence. He claims the purchasing power in the influence market is five to seven times greater than kids' primary purchase power. If this is true, the influence market in North America, based on our conservative estimates above, *could be worth $577 billion to $808 billion (U.S.).*

The future market is what kids will buy when they become adults. It is the end result of kids growing up in a consumer culture, making brand choices. The prize for business is the potential for the loyalty of the kids to translate into loyal adult customers. The economic impact of this segment cannot be quantified today but marketers know that brand loyalty is an important part of the equity that makes a brand valuable.

James McNeal considers the future market the largest segment of kidfluence and the one with the greatest potential since adult purchases drive most economies.

McNeal's segmentation is a great resource for those who are interested in kids and business. But it also provides a challenging perspective to the kid market because it recognizes and quantifies that the impact of kid consumers goes beyond what candy they like to the end result of what these consuming experiences may mean when they become adults. This is of real interest to all brand marketers who understand that the future health of their companies depends on strong brand equity carried into the future.

In the next few chapters we will explore kidfluence in action.

In Chapter 8 we will look at the primary kid market for examples of how kid businesses today are managing and growing and how new businesses are emerging.

In Chapter 9 we will analyse the power of influence and how and where it happens in families.

In Chapter 10 we will look into the future and project how branding and consumer experiences can form impressions that may last a lifetime.

In Chapter 11 we crystal-ball about the futures of Generation Y. What will they be like as adults when they grew up as savvy consumers?

So now when we think of the kid market we can ask—do you mean the $115 billion North American market of kids with their own discretionary income or do you mean the $600-plus billion market that they influence, or the market that they will become in 10 to 20 years' time? Any way you look at it, kids mean business.

8

Kids Buying Kid Stuff

I suppose you can't have everything,
though my instinctive reaction to
this sentiment is "why not?"
—*Margaret Halsey*

Because kids want to buy, many businesses are succeeding by meeting the needs and creating the must-haves for the kid market. We explore a few here—from the traditional kid businesses like licensed collectibles, toys and hot fashions to the newer businesses affected by the echo boom, such as movies, family packaged goods and banks. We will also explore the impact of kidfluence on the media and research and consulting firms which have all made it their business to know kids.

Kids Love Fashion
When researching this book it became apparent that if there was one business poised to cash in on the growth in the kid population it was the fashion business. Kids love clothes and love to spend money on them. The growth in tween and teen clothing businesses has been the talk of the retail industry for the last few years. Some sources claim that apparel is the fastest growing kid market. Specialty stores like Chickaboom in Toronto and mall retailers like La Senza and Suzy Shier are offering tweens their own stores and clothing lines.

In the U.S. most major retailers are expanding into kids' lines and expecting serious expansion and growth over the next couple of years. Some of the notable new lines in North America for both boys and girls include:

- Limited Too (from Limited)
- abercrombie (from Abercrombie & Fitch)
- Talbots Kids (from Talbots)
- La Senza Girl (from La Senza)
- Junior Girl (from Le Chateau)
- Roots Kids (from Roots)
- CMX (from Club Monaco)
- And the ones who lead the pack: Gap Kids and Gap Baby (from the Gap).

Established chain stores have a natural advantage when considering a jump onto the kid bandwagon, but some independent-minded merchants also stepped forward to ride the wave of the booming junior population. One store in Toronto that experienced success with tweens is Chickaboom. Chickaboom is a store that sells hip fashion and accessories to tween girls. They differentiated themselves by building a store that tween girls could really call their own. Chickaboom connects with their customers with special events like slumber parties and Spice Girl days. Their mailers are addressed personally to the girl, not her parents, and in-store staff is trained to make eye contact with the kid first, not the mother. Nancy Dennis, a former retail executive at the Bay and Eaton's, started the company in 1997 after reading David Foot's *Boom Bust & Echo*. "Tween girls was such an obvious niche that I had to do it." Dennis sensed the gap in the retail market and saw she could fill a customer need because tween girls were caught between kid and adult stores. Focusing on tweens was also a sounder business opportunity because the market was less competitive than the teen market. She approached many large companies but ended up starting the business on her own with one investor. In the first year sales were double her forecast, so she opened a second store in Yorkdale Mall in Toronto. The expansion proved that success came too fast and Dennis filed for bankruptcy when her overhead costs exceeded her ability to manage cash flow. "If I had stayed with one store I would have been fine. There have been a million knock-offs of Chickaboom since I started and it is difficult for a small store to compete." (At printing, Chickaboom is still in business with new owners.)

Dennis was right that more tween retailers are entering the market. The Limited, an American fashion company, created the Limited too to cater to girls 7–11 in the expectation that they would be "growing" a market for the women's line. Le Chateau, a trendy fashion retailer in Canada has approached the market a different way. Their Junior Girl line is targeted at girls, 8 to 14 years old, and is marketed as its own brand of clothing and accessories within the same store that sells fashions to teens and twenty-somethings. In its first year of business, Le Chateau reported the Junior Girls' line brought in $10 million of the stores' $160 million total in sales.

Tween girls are the darlings of the specialty store set but they aren't the only ones targeted by marketers out to capture the hearts and minds of kids to teens, including boys. Zellers, the well-known Canadian mass merchandiser with 320 stores, made two moves in 1999 to encourage kids and teens to shop at Zellers. The first was the introduction of a new line of clothing and accessories called Request. The second was to launch a loyalty program specifically for kids under 18.

Why did Zellers, who position themselves as Mom's store, want to attract kids? "Because kids are an important part of family shopping and being 'Mom's store' means we are really a family store. The more Zellers can do to help moms with their shopping needs the better. We also know that kids' and tweens' products sell well in our stores, so we thought we could grow that part of the business," says Peter Housley, who was the Senior Vice President of Marketing in 1999. Launching a known brand name was important to Zellers. Request was an established fashion brand in the U.S. to which Zellers gained exclusive rights in Canada. Marketers at Zellers believed that the Request brand name would provide brand credibility for tweens and teens, and that its streetwear and denim fashions would have high appeal with both genders.

The timing of the launch in August 1999 was a good thing and a bad thing. In back- to-school season every department store tries to attract the high-spending tweens and teens to their store. If you flip through the newspaper flyers in August you see each store trying to capture the "denim and denim-friendly" business. When Zellers decided to launch Request at this key retail selling period, they knew they had to do something different to break through the advertising clutter. The marketing team at Zellers and one of their communications partners named Zig, which is an ideas company based in Toronto, created an innovative promotion as the launch vehicle for the Request brand. The All Request Free CD promotion offered a free compilation CD for every $30 of Request product purchased. The CD showcased the hot dance tracks of Sony music stars and Zellers supported the promotion with outdoor, TV commercial, and eye-catching in-store displays. 280,000 CDs were given away and over $10 million in sales were achieved in the first five weeks of the launch, double the planned sales of $5 million.

"It was the most successful promotion and launch I had experienced in my career," claims Housley. "Kids were flocking to the stores to get the new clothes and CD."

So why was this such a success with kids? Andy Macaulay, a founding Zig partner, believes "one of the quickest ways to get an unknown brand on the radar screen of teens is to do it by association. For Request, we chose to introduce the brand to teens by associating it with music. Specifically, we gave them a custom compilation CD of very current music which they could only get from Request. The benefit was twofold: Request's association with music, and the fact that the brand gave the teens something very tangible."

The second step of the Zellers family plan was to reward kids as well as moms for shopping at their store. The Zellers Club Z program enjoys the position of being the first and the biggest loyalty program in Canada. In 1998, working again with Zig, Zellers built on the strength of Club Z and added the kid extension to the program. Generation Z was designed to benefit kids aged one to 18 when they or their moms (or dads) shopped at Zellers. The idea was that every time a Zellers adult shopper earned Club Z points they automatically earned Gen Z points for their kids on the same purchase. If kids bought, they earned points themselves. In effect, Zellers gave double points to the household, but the kids got their own points catalogue to choose from and the chance to redeem them for cool products like watches, electronics and movie passes. Zellers believes the Generation Z program is the first of its kind, and it was considered a success when it signed up one million kids in its first year. While every member helps make Generation Z stronger, Andy Macaulay thinks it is the tweens that will contribute the most to Zellers' success with the loyalty program.

"Our analysis led us to target the 7 to 12 age group as the primary audience for Gen Z. They were old enough to exert substantial influence on their parents' choice of store, but young enough that they weren't going off to shop on their own as older teens do. The result was maximum influence on the household's spending."

Zellers has been able to track the success of this program and has discovered that Generation Z households spent 17 per cent more at Zellers once they became Gen Z members. "This is a significant lift in our business and it proves the power of the kid influence in the family shopping behaviour," says Peter Housley. Beyond the increased sales, Zellers now also has a comprehensive kid-to-teen database, putting them in an advantageous position as these kids grow into Zellers' "moms."

Given the tweens' aversion to department and drug stores there is a huge opportunity for a company to make a difference in those environments. One department store that tried to woo the tween and teen in Canada was Eaton's department store. In summer 1998, as part of their positioning to be the leading fashion retailer in Canada, they launched a department called Diversity. Diversity was an entire floor of the Toronto flagship Eaton's Centre store devoted to teens. In smaller stores and markets Diversity was a unique section on the same floor as other departments.

Eaton's put an emphasis on the teens for three reasons. First the company wanted a fair share of the teen market. They observed that specialty retailers were being successful with the fashionable teen target, and their own retail experience had proven it was a lucrative market. Second, they needed to grow the future clientele of Eaton's, as the median age of their current customer base was over 40. And third, but possibly most importantly, they believed that keeping their finger on the pulse of the junior market was crucial to being a legitimate fashion leader. "Fashionable teens were another piece of proof that Eaton's was a fashion store. It was the first salvo in the new war," says John Miller of Toronto, a key player in the repositioning and launch of Diversity.

Diversity was meant to be more than a clothing department. It was designed to be a destination. Research told Eaton's that kids wanted to have an environment where they were welcome, an environment where they could hang out and spend time with their friends and not be treated like criminals. Kids and teens up to this point felt uncomfortable in department stores. Carolyn Meacher, an Eaton's marketing executive at the time, said changing the stores' attitudes towards the teens was critical. "Teens had been mistreated by the stores. They were treated like shoplifters or vagrants. They needed to feel like they belonged. The qualitative research during concept development helped the internal team at Eaton's come to the same point of view." While Eaton's research told them that kids didn't start with a positive view of department stores because they had been dragged to the stores by their parents for years, Diversity's product and merchandising in the end made them see Eaton's as a cool destination.

Unfortunately, this new venture was short-lived. Diversity was launched in August 1998, but by February 1999 Eaton's was in serious financial trouble, culminating in bankruptcy in the spring. The six months' business results for Diversity demonstrated to those involved that "Diversity was more than an experiment—it was growing into a little success story," with sales 20 to 30 per cent ahead of those forecast in the three downtown locations.

Macy's, the U.S. department store, is testing a new "junior department" environment in San Francisco. The test store was revamped with exposed ceilings, a new D.J. booth, and staff that are true to their cohort with coloured hair and pierced body parts. Reports claim the junior department has increased sales by 19 per cent and Macy's is planning on rolling out the new format to possibly 75 stores in 2001.

The Internet is also the perfect way to capture retail spending with tweens and teens. As we discussed in Chapter 4: The Wired World, today's kids are a digitally savvy group who have grown up with a mouse in their hands, making them a natural and enthusiastic audience for Web shopping.

But when it comes to shopping on-line there is a barrier to the kid business. Kids are cash rich and the world of e-commerce is not a cash environment. YouthCulture, a youth media and research company in Toronto, found in their Teen Internet Study released in

What Makes Kids Like a Store?

- Kid-friendly atmosphere—they like kids
- Kid products
- Eye-level displays
- Communication with kids
- Others like it

Source: James McNeal, *Kids as Customers*

Spring 2000 that of the 55 per cent of teens that were shopping on-line, only 10 per cent were buying, due to lack of credit cards. But even this barrier can be overcome by kidfluence.

In the U.S., where buying by catalogue and on the Internet is more developed than in Canada, companies are discovering that kids will find a way to buy what they want. Cyber Dialogue is an Internet consultancy that claims that 10 per cent of teens have their own credit cards and 9 per cent have access to a parent's card to shop on-line. But for those who don't have plastic, several e-commerce sites have emerged to solve the problem. Sites like icanbuy.com and rocketcash.com allow parents to set up e-commerce accounts for their kids where they can spend on credit cards to preset limits or have their own debit accounts paid for by money order or cheque. Then the kids can spend preset amounts with participating merchants and parents don't fear huge credit card bills. And with kids spending so much cash it is not surprising that VISA has developed a special credit card for teens. The VISA Buxx card works like a prepaid phone card and can be used wherever VISA is accepted. Parents can apply for the cards and load them with cash through VISA's Web site.

Delias is one on-line store where the small issue of cash has not stopped them from being a huge success. Launched in 1994, Delias is one of the hottest names in Generation Y retailing due to its customer passion and its rising stock price. Delias offers clothing and accessories to girls aged 8 to 17 through a unique grassroots catalogue-drop system and Web presence. Delias customers use their own or their parents' credit cards or use the debit services of doughnet and rocketcash. With this access they can tap into the wallets as well as the mindset of the tween girl.

Delias is seen to be unique because it defines its business by its customers, not its product. Delias speaks the language of its customers and reaches them where they live—though catalogues in schoolyards—not in the traditional method of mass marketing. Building on their success, the company is now branching out into other offerings like home furnishings and retailing to boys. As they have grown they have seen the benefits of venturing into mass media to broaden their reach to more customers. The owners want to stay close to their customers, using whatever media strategy it takes, because the owners see their businesses growing up with their customers: "As they need a credit card, car loan and mortgage we will follow them and broaden our offerings." The Delias case study gives more information. (See case studies at the back of the book for full report.)

It is hard to be in the fashion business without feeling the impact of teen culture. Teens have both the independence and the larger budgets to support teen-focused businesses. Brands have become an important part of teen culture, of identity. David Elkind, the author of *All Grown Up and No Place to Go*, says that it is increasingly through fads and fashions that adolescents come together. Marketers expert at targeting this age group talk of teen tribes to describe the segmentation of the teen world. Each tribe has a look, and brands play an important role in creating the desirability of that look. One retailer who understood the need for a "tribe look" was the Limited, when they revamped the store Abercrombie & Fitch in the United States. Abercrombie & Fitch had 230 stores in 1999 with revenues of $816 million U.S. It has been the darling of the retail analysts, with 29 straight quarters of growth reported at the end of 1999. How did Abercrombie do it? They took a tired preppy look and made it hip, they hired the coolest, best-looking kids to work at their stores and they launched a catalogue that celebrated the lifestyle of "the abercrombie crew." Faded jeans and T-shirts, rumpled shirts and cargo pants became the hot preppy athletic looks of this generation. This very popular tribe look is now targeted toward the younger set with the launch of abercrombie (note the lowercase letters designating kids rather than teens) in 1999. Specialty stores, like Abercrombie & Fitch, captured 44 per cent of the $4.6 billion U.S. that teens spent on clothing last year according to the retail tracking firm NPD Group. Department stores got only 13 per cent of the teen spending—which shows that with kids you have to have the right merchandise and the right environment to make them want to spend their money. Department stores are not a preferred destination for teens, regardless of the brands they offer, because they are not relevant to them. While the product is important, to be a successful retailer the whole shopping experience needs to appeal to the teens. Given the power of kids and teens, department stores could be losing out on a whole generation.

The world of fashion is one of the hot primary markets to feel kidfluence. There are several other traditional primary markets where kids are spending more and more.

Toys and Collectibles

The toy business is a big kid business. In the United States $22 billion are spent every year on toys, and the greatest influence on what gets bought is from kids.

FAO Schwartz is synonymous with toys in the United States. Their flagship store in Manhattan routinely draws huge crowds that are willing to line up and wait to enter the store. Based on their niche in the toy world, one can assume that if anyone knows kids and toys it is FAO. So if FAO has determined that tweens are a unique market, it must be true. FAO Schwartz has set up FAO Girl boutiques in some of their stores to appeal to tween girls who may not be interested in the rest of the toy store. "We caught the trend late in 1998," explains a merchant with the store. FAO saw the chance to capitalize on the "girl power" theme made popular by the British band the Spice Girls and are attempting to capture the child who is not "into" Barbie any more. The FAO Girl concept is selling a "lifestyle," rather than individual products, to 7- to 12-year-olds. The line includes writing sets, personal accessories and collectible items. FAO Girl can be found in all 42 FAO locations. In the smallest store the brand is displayed separately at the end of an aisle, but in the New York flagship store 200 to 400 square feet are dedicated to the concept. FAO Schwartz continues to build on their strength in the kid market with the introduction in 2000 of FAO Baby. The focus for the baby line is to offer unique gifts and home and personal furnishings for infants to toddlers.

When we think of toys many of us think of dolls. Dolls are an important part of growing up, especially for girls. One company that has made girls and their dolls their focus and mission is the Pleasant Company's American Girls Collection. Pleasant Rowland created the American Girls collection for American girls aged 7 to 12 to provide girls with "rich, age-appropriate play experiences," states the company's brochure. Rowland was an educator who wanted to give modern girls an understanding of America's past and a sense of pride in their traditions. The American Girl collection is almost exclusively available though the company's catalogue in the United States.

This particular "rich play experience" has a price tag to match. Whereas Barbies can be owned for $20-30, an American Girl doll and a couple of outfits with accessories will cost well above $200 U.S. Most doll

Kids Change the Book Business

The success of the Harry Potter series, the books starring the young wizard created by U.K. writer J. K. Rowling for kids in primary and junior grades, surprised everyone in the book business. A book is a best-seller in Canada when it sells 5,000 copies. The first three titles in the Harry Potter series have sold more than a million copies in Canada and at the time of writing (July 2000), 300,000 copies of the fourth title in the series, *Harry Potter and Goblet of Fire,* had been printed for launch in July 2000. An article in the *Globe and Mail* reported that booksellers are ecstatic about kids being interested in books. One claims that in 20 years she has never seen so many children and adults excited about

(Continued on next page)

owners own more than one doll and the accessory collection is designed around each doll's own activities and interests. The "need for more" is encouraged through the many business channels operated by the Pleasant Company. They reach their doll owners through their magazine, their books and catalogues. These old-fashioned dolls are marketed with leading-edge retail savvy, exemplified by the launch of American Girl Place in downtown Chicago just off the Magnificent Mile. American Girl Place is 35,000 square feet of girl heaven. It is a doll, book, accessory and clothing store, with a restaurant, a photo studio and a live musical theatre revue all celebrating the American Girls Collection. American Girls is such a hit with affluent American girls that their parents take them on pilgrimages to the shrine of their heroines—their dolls. The launch of this retail theatre builds on the success of selling more than 4 million dolls and 48 million books since 1986. The bimonthly *American Girl* magazine with 750,000 subscribers and an estimated two million readers makes American Girl bigger than most Canadian adult magazines. And while the company has been built on commendable virtues that encourage a love of history and genuine American values, the sheer display of mass consumerism at American Girl Place is overwhelming to those not familiar with the doll phenomenon. A childless adult visitor commented while visiting Chicago Place that the "cultlike" zeal to wrap up the visitors in everything American Girl was a little disheartening. This marketing-on-overdrive is very apparent in the souvenir memory book called My Day at American Girl Place. In this book girls are encouraged to purchase in powerful prose. An excerpt: "As you look around the boutique, pick up special tickets for the treasures you wish you could have. If you're lucky, maybe you'll leave the store with some of them tucked in a bright berry-colored bag." The "berry-colored bag" is the shopping bag for American Girl Place and a sign of a successful trip for most of the young girls visiting there. American Girl is a traditional kid business that has definitely made a new success out of kidfluence and kid affluence.

Pokémon is a phenomenal trend that swept North America in the late 1990s. It is a collectible business that has something for everyone. What makes it such a huge business and phenomenon is that it covers every kid business imaginable, from trading cards, toys

Kids Change the Book Business
(Continued from previous page)

a book. "We've been losing market share to other media and now there's this author who has created a whole new generation of readers. Harry Potter has brought people back to reading."

Thirty million copies of Harry Potter sold around the world is a sure sign of kidfluence in action.

and books, T-shirts and backpacks, to movies and electronic games. If you have kids you have Pokémon merchandise in your home because, surprisingly, these "pocket monsters" attract both boys and girls from preschool to tweens. The market for most toys and games is segmented by gender and age group. Pokémon has breadth because younger kids love Pokémon cards and toys, while the video game is in demand with the 8-and-older group. The Nintendo Pokémon Gameboy has really put a dent in kids' pocketbooks in the past few years, with 11 million games having been sold worldwide. At Christmas 1999 a Yellow Gameboy could not be found on retail shelves, as schoolyard buzz had made it "the" item kids had to have. As the buzz grew, so did Pokémon merchandise to include videos, books, sticker sets and two movies. All this adds up to $6 billion U.S. in sales. According to the *Big Blue Dot Trend Reporter*, a newsletter that provides information on kid trends in North America, sales in the video game segment of the toy business are reaching all-time highs and the portables category increased 50 per cent as a result of the popularity of the Pokémon games and GameBoy colour versions.

Some adults think the Pokémon craze happened overnight, but like most kid trends it was fully entrenched by the time the adults caught up with it. "I don't believe that kids' phenomena are due to sales and marketing. Phenomena usually build in the kids' network, travelling by word of mouth," claims children's writer and media critic Kathleen McDonnell. While parents may love it or hate it most are indifferent because it is just one more in a series of fads that the kids go through. "Last year it was Crazy Bones, then it was Star Wars ... they are all just excuses to spend money," one mom laments.

The Movies

Tweens are making their way into the world and how they look is an important part of the person they are becoming. But shopping and dressing is only one passion. Kids this age start to get out on their own as well and one industry that has been transformed in North America by the youth market is "the movies." Kids and young adults 12 to 20 make up 16 per cent of the population in the U.S., but they buy 26 per cent of the movie tickets. With these types of statistics, kids are having an effect on everything from what gets made in Hollywood to the venues where the movies are being shown. Teens have traditionally loved going to movies, and now kids are growing up with the movie theatre being part of their regular experience. "My kids know when movies are coming out and expect to go on opening weekend. And once is not enough, we have to see the movie in the theatre over and over again just as if it were a video," says one exasperated mother. Box-office numbers support this scenario, and with opening weekend receipts determining the success or failure of a movie, kids and teens can make or break it. Witness the *Titanic* phenomenon, where Leo Di Caprio's fans needed to see him as many as 10 times at the theatre. "The studios have always been interested in kids because they buy toys that are licensed (which expands the market opportunity cross-category sales from the movies to toys to lunch boxes to clothing) but the tide has turned since *Titanic* came out. The story goes that one billion of the total box office was teen-derived from multiple viewings," says Ken Faier, executive vice-president publishing director of the kid-based media company Brunico communications in 1999, who publish *Kidscreen* magazine, among other things.

With numbers like that you can understand why Hollywood has spawned teen-movie specialist divisions and kid and teen hit movies spawn sequels within a year or two (Think *Scream* and *Toy Story*). One executive refused to call the recent success of kid movies a trend. He believes that families are just looking for family activities, and if there is a family movie available parents will take their kids to see it. Again this is a sign of the different family relationships we see with boomers and their kids. They want to spend fun time together and going to a movie is an easy way to please everyone. If you look at the run of hit kid/family movies from November 1999 into the early months of 2000—from *Pokémon The Movie* to *The Tigger Movie*, *Stuart Little*, *Toy Story 2*, and *Dinosaur*— you would see ticket grosses from $85 million to the high of *Toy Story 2* at $240 million, and that is a trend definitely being fuelled by kidfluence.

Beyond the actual show, the whole experience of seeing a movie has also changed. The theatre is now an entertainment complex where you can eat, drink, lounge and play interactive games, as well as catch a flick. And the desire to capture that family activity is driving the changes. Famous Players Canada's largest theatre chain is spending $400 million opening 30 multiplex complexes in hopes of capitalizing on the interest of kids, youth and boomers who want a break from cocooning. This level of entertainment is also a new trend in shopping malls. Shoppertainment has lead some retail mall developers to call them "nightclubs for kids." But both the mall and the movie theatre trends are tapping into the kid-fuelled entertainment market, which is driven by families who want a place to go, where they can spend their precious leisure time together and all get to do an activity they like. The entertainment environment is also the new choice of hangout for teens who like to be where the action is. And parents

---

Did You Know ...

Each year, Teen girls in the U.S. spend $4 billion US on cosmetics?

Teens in the U.S. spend $12.7 billion at U.S. fast-food restaurants?

The average teen eats 4.33 times a day, one-third of it away from home?

47% of first in-store requests by children is for cereal

30% of first in-store requests is for snack items—candy, cookies, frozen desserts

---

21% of first in-store requests is for toys

Teenscreen Special report
James McNeal, "Born to Shop," *American Demographics*, June 1993

seem to like knowing where their kids are spending their time and seem happy to drop off Jennifer and her friends at the "megaplex" for a couple of hours. The changing world of kidfluence is evident in both of these environments.

Kidfluence Creates New Businesses

In recent years the kid market has been legitimized by the introduction of many new kid products. Many packaged goods once considered family purchases are now bought solely for the kids. Toothpaste that sparkles and toothbrushes with cartoon characters, fruity shampoos and school lunch packs are just a few of the examples of new businesses that have been created as a direct response to the pull of the kid market. One boomer mother relates: "When my five-year-old son called out to me in the drugstore with 'Mommy, there's my shampoo—don't forget to buy that,' I knew the world had changed. He picked out this L'Oreal kid shampoo with the fuschia bottle and the orange cap. He had never seen it before or tried it—but he knew it was for him. When I asked him how he knew that it was for him he looked at me like I was crazy. 'It's obvious Mom,' he said, 'the colours are cool and I know it is going to smell great.'"

This is kidfluence in action. Kids know what they like and what they want, and if they don't have the money themselves they just ask an adult to buy it for them. Some marketers cling to the notion that advertising drives kidfluence, but more and more "decisions" by kids are happening in-store, on the spot. We know that more families are shopping together in an effort to both save time and share time, and this opportunity allows kids to see and ask for new things.

Like the child who spotted the new shampoo, kids react to choices directly in front of them. They are true impulse shoppers because they don't rationalize price or need. A kid's world is a world of immediate gratification. Just walk down any aisle in the grocery store and you can see the tactics of kid marketers who are trying to appeal to this spontaneity. Kids respond to colours, type styles and character designs. These are the signals that fuel the kid primary market. The checkout aisle is primary market heaven. You have a captive child, a tired and distracted mother ... and the result? More than a few candy purchases.

The primary market is further expanded when non-traditional businesses become effected by kidfluence. Financial services is a business where kids don't seem like an obvious business opportunity. But if you have money you also need somewhere to keep it other than under the bed. So kids need and do use banks. In the 1999 *YTV Kid & Tween Report*, 63 per cent of tweens claim to have a bank account and 19 per cent use a bank card. Tweens also save. They save for electronics, sports, clothing or music. In the USA *Weekend Teens & Money Survey*, two-thirds of teens surveyed say they have saved in the last week and only 8 per cent say they are not saving at all. This survey found that teens were sensitized to the importance of money in their lives. Four out of five teens consider themselves financially savvy. They link having money to their future success in getting a good education and in life. When asked what they would do if they were given $100, almost half (48 per cent) said they would save or invest it, with boys slightly more likely to save than spend.

Banks and investment companies are starting to make contact with this younger audience. CIBC sponsored the 1999 *YTV Kid & Tween Report* so they could understand the kid market better and plan for the future. *Canadian Business* magazine reported on the kid market in an article in 1998 and showed a chart that listed four banks, including the CIBC, and a mutual fund company as having special kid programs. In Quebec the Caisses Populaire Desjardins encourages kids to open bank accounts with an initiative called "bas de laine" which literally means wool sock. This saying is in reference to a French-Canadian tradition of *saving* your money (historically in socks) versus investing in stocks. "Today's young people are more fiscally able-minded," says Stein Roe of Young Investors Fund. This American investment company has catered to the under-17 age group since it started in 1994. About 85 per cent of the fund's 200,000 shareholders are under 17. The average investor is 11. Stein Roe's parent company Liberty Financial has a Web site for kids called younginvestor.com, where kids can learn about money and investing. And they are certainly learning. A recent article in the *Wall Street Journal* claimed that 35 per cent of eighth—twelfth graders owned stocks or bonds and one-fifth owned mutual funds. Prior to the nineties, stock ownership in the under 20 group, was essentially zero.

Money influences how kids feel about the world and kids money influences how the world feels about them. This symbiotic relationship is what adds up to the power of kidfluence. But today's money is not the big prize to these companies. It is Gen Y's future money, when they are working adults and when they inherit from their boomer parents, that will benefit those financial companies that reached out to them as kids.

Kids' Home Fashion

Kids today want cool-looking bedrooms. Some kids, if their parents are divorced, even have two rooms to think about. It means that home furnishings is also a new kid business. In previous generations kids got the hand-me-down furniture that was available but today kids and tweens want their rooms to express who they are. IKEA understood this desire when they got tweens and teens to design their ideal bedrooms for a contest. The winners won their rooms and got to see their designs displayed in the stores. IKEA is an all-family store that understands the new style of family living today. They also recognized that tweens were a niche opportunity to drive new sales volume and influence their families to visit IKEA.

Other home furnishing retailers are now beginning to focus only on kids. Pottery Barn, a home store in the U.S., launched Pottery Barn Kids after they watched the success that clothing retailers in the States were having with the tween target. Pottery Barn initially launched a catalogue to test the business idea but quickly moved to launching stores. Stores as diverse as Ethan Allen furniture (with an EA kid's line) and Nestings Kids in Toronto are all trying to capitalize on the demands of stylish kids and the willingness of parents to fund those demands.

Another traditional adult business that has turned to kidfluence is Kodak, the camera and film company. To grow beyond their current business Kodak has put girls aged 9 to 15 in their sights. The company wants this new generation to own Kodak digital cameras and is attempting to capture their interest with promotions that link the brand to young performers like Youngstown, another "cute boys" singing group. Research showed that among tween girls the most prized possessions were their photographs and Tween girls like to "archive." They collect pictures, photographs and ticket stubs and maintain journals to connect

The peak of the echo boom is just turning 10 years old and will be a viable market for quite some time.

with and remember their experiences. Targeting tweens gives Kodak business growth today while also building the market of the future by reaching tweens through their natural interest in their products and brands. Robert Deutsch, a cognitive anthropologist and consultant at DDB Needham Advertising in New York, believes that "if you can help people realize the novelty of themselves as individuals you can apply your brand viscerally in their lives to enhance loyalty over time." Kids as new business opportunities should not be dismissed as just kid stuff. With the peak of the echo boom just turning 10 in 2000, kids appear to be a healthy market for a while yet.

Making Kids a Business

We have discussed the primary market where kids spend their own money and ask their parents for more money to the tune of $115 billion and more. But not surprisingly, given the dollars and interest involved in the kid market, another business segment has flourished: service businesses that focus on the business of kids, businesses that exist solely to help businesses reach kids. These businesses profit by teaching people about the benefits of the kid market, create marketing and advertising plans specially targeted to kids and develop media vehicles to reach kids.

FIGURE 1 *Tweens Say "Given $100, I Would..."*

BOYS		GIRLS
55%	Save/Invest it	45%
19%	Buy clothes	50%
25%	Buy electronics/software	12%
5%	Give it to others	7%
10%	Buy sporting goods	3%

Source: YTV Kid & Tween Report, *1999*.

Ken Faier, of Brunico Communications in 1999, a company that publishes kid magazines and holds marketing conferences focused on the youth market, states that "when we launched *Kidscreen* magazine [a kid trade magazine serving the entertainment industry] in 1996 there was no other magazine like ours, and there were no conferences geared to kids. Now there is a saturation in the number of conferences about marketing to kids. There are probably 10–12 companies in North America a year doing conferences about kids because of the growth in the sector." Brunico holds three conferences about youth a year. Researchers for *Kidfluence* attended one of their conferences in Phoenix in 1999 and were surprised at the breadth of interest in the subject matter from manufacturers, marketers, media people and advertising executives in attendance.

"Today there is more and more media targeting kids, thanks to the growth of networks in the U.S. like Cartoon Network, Nickelodeon, Disney, UPN, and Fox Family Network," says Ken Faier.

In Canada the kid media has had success as well. YTV is a kid network that broadcasts YTV and Treehouse TV. The company started in 1988 and has grown leaps and bounds over the years, according to Suzanne Carpenter, the vice president of sales. "YTV started in 4 million households in Canada and grew very quickly. It is now in 8 million households or 96 per cent of Canada." But their media reach with kids does not end with their TV shows. YTV launched a Web site in 1997 and a kid magazine called *Whoa!* in 1999. "Both of these are wonderful opportunities to extend the brand," says Susan Schaefer, VP Marketing YTV. "We also get out with a travelling roadshow called WOW—for Weird on Wheels—and that allows us to interact with the kids." YTV has really connected with kids because surveys show that Canadian kids watch YTV more than any other channel. And of course YTV wants this connection to grow with ideas for more media channels like a radio station, and their own CD titled *BigFunPartyMix*. (See the case studies at the back of the book for a full report.)

With media vehicles that need advertising revenue, there are plenty of advertising and marketing consultants who are ready and able to help marketers communicate with kids. Kid marketing and communication is considered a specialty in the advertising world. And since the kids have become such a buying force the expertise on how to reach them is even more desirable. *Advertising Age* is a trade publication for the marketing and advertising industry in the United States; every year it does a special report on marketing to youth. In February 2000, it highlighted 12 companies whose sole business is helping other companies with their kid marketing. Six of these companies had been operating for less than three years and entered the field because of the impact of kidfluence. Many of the world's biggest advertising agencies have launched a kid division because they believe kid culture is unique and merits the undivided attention of a dedicated division. Most companies have proprietary research to give them insights into the kid world. "The fact that kids are learning and growing puts a very different spin on whatever you do for them, compared to what you do for adults," says one executive. And where there is advertising there are award shows. The "Golden Marble" is an annual award for the best advertising to kids in North America, and it is hosted by *Kidscreen* magazine, from Brunico Communications. In 1999 there were over 350 entries, proving that kidfluence also wants to be noticed.

In Canada there are several companies who consider themselves experts on kids marketing and research. Many were contacted as resources for this book, including DDBkidthink, Environics, Generations Research, In-Sync, Leo Burnett/KidLeo, MINA, the NRG Group, and Youth Culture. Each company has a perspective on how to talk to kids and what makes them special consumers and communication targets.

Greg Skinner, Director of MINA, a market research company in Toronto for customers under 35, believes there are special challenges to marketing to kids. He states that because prestige and status are important themes when reaching kids "a brand must develop the esteem that will interest them." He adds that kids are also fickle, so it is difficult to keep up with them. Companies like MINA help marketers understand what kids are into and develop messages that will appeal to them. MINA helped Eaton's understand the different "tribes" of teens when the department store wanted to build the teen Diversity department in 1998. MINA described 16 distinct tribes, that each with its own mindset and fashion approach. This segmentation was designed to help Eaton's better target the teens and connect successfully with them to interest them in Eaton's new department. Teen tribes have increased over the last few decades. In the 1970s and 1980s most kids could be classified as jocks, rockers, preppies or geeks but by the year 2000 teen tribes are more fragmented. "Niche marketing is more 'in' than it has ever been," according to Sean Saraq formerly co-director of Environics Youth Research Division, and now a partner in Youth Culture, "because of growing [developing] social values and stylistic fragmentations among the young, and simply because of technological advances and a proliferation of media venues that make it easier to target smaller groups of individuals." MINA called the phenomenon "cross pollination" because the tribes are becoming harder to identify when kids are far more willing to experiment and accept influences outside their immediate reference group.

Other experts don't agree with the tribe approach to teen marketing. Max Valiquette of the NRG Group, a Toronto-based youth marketing advisory service, says tribes are a trap and that marketers are fooling themselves because they won't reach youth with this type of segmentation. Cameron Smith from the research company The Angus Reid Group would agree, when he says the lines between tribes aren't as clear-cut as they sometimes appear and that teens can borrow from many different influences. Valiquette believes it makes more sense to focus on teen commonalities rather than their differences. The new trend is toward understanding teen values and developing psychographic profiles, because while teens may experiment with many different fashion and style statements and have different interests they can still share the same values. Discovering and tracking these teen values goes beyond looking for what is "cool." A lot of teen research and marketing is about "cool hunting"—discovering what is really hot and trying to attach a product or brand to that trend. The NRG Group believes teens can see through that superficial approach. As Valiquette says, "If you are doing cool, you are always trying to chase who other people think you should be rather than being true to a brand's values. Kids know when something is authentic."

Being in touch with the changing tastes and trends of tweens and teens is hard work, and companies where teens and tweens are their only focus need to check in with their audience constantly. YTV, the kid TV channel, works with In-Sync, a consumer planning and research company in Toronto, to help them stay in touch with the tween world. Together they developed a kid panel, which has helped YTV better understand their mindset. "Seeing the kids makes a big difference," says Director of Marketing Laura Baehr. "Watching a kid scrunch up their face in reaction to something—you don't get that out of a written research report. Visiting with the panel is very immediate, and in the moment—we get to stay in touch on a more regular basis." YTV uses many forms of research, including the large tracking study referred to in this book, and focus groups, but the panel gives them a regular, up-to-the-minute reading on the state of kid culture. "Kids are our business—

we have to be on top of what kids are doing and thinking. A panel may not be right for everyone but it compliments all the efforts we make," says Baehr. (See case study at the back of the book for full report.)

Reaching Kids in School

Since kids spend most of their day in school, marketers see schools as a desirable, and new medium through which to reach kids. Schools spell opportunity for Paton Marketing Services, a Canadian company that brings corporations and schools together by developing social marketing programs geared towards kids. Bev Paton started the company in 1994 with an environment magazine called *POP* (*POP* stands for Protecting our Planet).

"*POP* is a vehicle where corporations with a socially responsible message that is of value to children can marry it with educational materials that meet curriculum guidelines and have it presented in the classroom as part of a teacher's course." A brochure describes *POP*'s mission as "to inspire kids to speak out and be heard and to take action on issues that concern them."

Social marketing isn't a new business, but with the growing desire to reach kids in more ways, given their economic clout, it is another opportunity for enlightened companies to connect with their prime targets. Understand-ably, some parents and educators may not like the corporate link to the classroom. Corporations in the classrooms became big news in the U.S. when television and videos with advertising sponsorship were brought into the school system, and in Canada when some schools made exclusive vending-machine deals with Pepsi. But those involved in social marketing believe their materials do not harm the children or act as corporate advertising. In fact they believe everyone benefits: the schools benefit with fresh materials and interesting relevant activities for the kids to do and learn from, and businesses get to give something back and promote the causes they believe in. One subject matter that everyone wanted to be involved with was the environment. The genesis of the classroom connection began with a desire by all to make social change through the kids. Paton cautions marketers to understand that her programs are not about sales but they achieve "a link to brand recognition, that your company cares about the same things that kids care about." The programs are not advertising, states

Recognizing the magnitude of kids' opinions, businesses are taking advantage of special conferences to learn more about this special market.

Paton. "We are very careful with how we go about creating a program. We do not take direct advertising, and it is not an obvious advertising promotion. We work with educators who develop the material for us and the program follows three principles: 1. It has to be fun for kids (otherwise they won't do it) 2. It has to be meaningful (so they learn something) and 3. It has to be actionable (so they do something with the experience)." An example of the type of program that *POP* supports is a Favourite Family Recipe Contest for Kraft. The *POP* program components included having kids send in their favourite family recipes, and the classroom activity taught fun food facts with the students learning about Canada's Food Guide.

Social marketing and kids is one more example of how the world of kids has changed even in the last two decades. When you talk with

Shop Around the World

The A.B.C. Global Kids Study is a survey of 2,400 kids aged seven to 12 and their mothers in China, France, Germany, Japan, the United Kingdom and the United States. It reports that kids in these countries lead similar lives and share many of the same interests and activities.

Consumerism is hot in all the countries polled, while saving is more popular in the east. Kids in the U.S. are the busiest shoppers with 55 per cent reporting shopping as a favourite activity; they are the biggest spenders, saving only 21 per cent of their monthly income:

Country	% Claim Shopping is Favourite Activity	Most Frugal % Income Saved Monthly
United States	55	21
Japan	47	62
China	46	60
British	37	
French	37	
Germany	37	

Source: Published in *American Demographics*, June 1997
To learn more about the A.B.C. Study, contact JustKid Inc.

adults who grew up in the 1960s and 1970s they are hard pressed to think of examples of kid issues or social causes that they were aware of at that time. "The environment wasn't an issue then the way it is now, and besides, we were shielded from most things by adults. It would have been something the adults handled not the kids—where today we get the kids involved when it does matter to them and their future," says one boomer parent.

So kidfluence is about more than buying and selling, it is also about kids wanting to have a say about things that affect their lives, present and future. Kidfluence is about parents and teachers who are open to giving them the stage to express their views. And if kids' views didn't matter, these business opportunities would not be a reality. Businesses would not be attending conferences to learn more about kids if they didn't think it meant business.

SPEED READ SUMMARY

The big news today is that the 88 million kids in North America mean big business because they have their own money and they are spending it everyday. This phenomenon is transforming businesses, from redefining traditional kid businesses to creating new opportunities.

- Kids have their own money and it's more than you may think. North American kids aged 4–19 are spending $115 billion a year.
- Kids spend their money where they want to and they don't like department and drug stores.
- Retailers are recognizing the importance of kids and developing separate lines, brands, stores just for them.
- Kids are impacting entertainment businesses, not only kid movies but all family entertainment choices.

- Kid businesses now include all family packaged goods like toothpaste and shampoo, as well as traditional adult businesses such as financial services, banking and investing.
- Specialized marketing has emerged to help businesses reach the kid market. Major advertising companies are launching separate divisions to specialize on youth. Kid experts can help businesses understand kids better and connect with them.

9

Kids Influencing Family Purchases

Money changes people just
as often as it changes hands
—*Al Balt*

Kids do buy on their own with their own money, but beyond the primary market is the impact of kids influencing more purchases by getting their parents to buy other things for them and the family. *The influence market*, five to seven times the size of the primary market according to one source and up to ten times that amount YTV calculates, impacts businesses far beyond any traditional notion of a "kid business." With $600 billion U.S. up for grabs businesses need to understand how kids influence the family purchases and where they influence the most. This chapter will share a few studies that illuminate the subtleties of influence.

Kids influence different purchases in different ways. Some appeals take the form of supermarket-aisle entreaties: "But, Mom, I *have* to have the neon crispy critters that turn the milk lime-green!" Others are inserted more soberly in family discussions about bigger purchases and represent a vote at the family table.

The Nag—Giving In Means Big Business

Pant-pulling, whining and persistent urging are examples of kidfluence in its most basic form. The nag factor is a big factor in business today. And while its sounds like creating an annoyance this annoyance is big business.

Every parent has heard "pleeaasse...I *need* it..." And while parents might say nagging doesn't work, a survey called "The Nag Factor" done in 1998–99, by Western International Media Corp., the largest media management company in the United States, indicates that between 20 and 40 per cent of the sales of toys, fast food and apparel are the result of kids' successful appeals to their parents.

FIGURE 1 **What Do Kids Ask For?**

Toys	89%
Movies	68%
Home Videos	64%
Theme Parks	64%
Cereals	55%
Snacks	53%
Beverages	44%
CD-ROMs	17%

Source: *"The Nag Factor," 1998–99, Western International Media Corp.*

Gene Del Vecchio has spent his career advertising to children, advising companies like Disney and Kraft and Mattel how to be successful with kids, and he is the author of the book *Creating Ever Cool: A Marketer's Guide to a Kid's Heart*. Del Vecchio calls this influence "Pester Power." He believes that Pester Power makes a big difference to a brand. He writes in his book that "kids' influence in the marketplace is such that businesses that do not listen to children's opinions will not reach their full potential and many will assuredly fail."

"Nag Factor"

The Western International Media Corp. survey revealed that most parents would prefer to go to Burger King or Pizza Hut rather than

McDonald's. But Pester Power takes them to McDonald's. This dynamic has made McDonald's one of the most successful businesses in the world, and young kids' number-one choice for a meal. Parents busy with juggling jobs and other responsibilities respond to their kids' wishes because they want to please and indulge them.

But what was revealing in this study was that in some categories the nagging mattered more because the parents claimed they would *not have bought* the item if the kids had not asked for it. This makes a big difference to a business person who may assume that adult awareness or distribution, or even the pricing of an item, is enough to elicit a sales response. Without that extra yank on the sleeve almost 50 per cent of parents would not purchase the toy, or 30 per cent of parents would not get the movie (see Figure 2). In business, nagging translates as a potential incremental lift in sales. Imagine increasing sales in CD-ROMs by 33 per cent just by getting the kids to nag for them?

FIGURE 2 **Nagging in Action**

Purchases that would not have been made if parents weren't nagged	
Toys	46%
Movies	34%
Food	34%
CD-ROMS	33%
Home Video	32%
Theme Parks	20%

Source: *"The Nag Factor" 1998–99, Western International Media Corp.*

Two Types of Nagging

Nagging, as our kids might tell us, is not a simple business. It can take on two forms: *persistent* and *importance* nagging.

Persistent nagging is the most annoying kind, where the request is repeated with increasing volume and intensity over time. Persistent nagging is the noise you frequently hear in toy stores and the sound that gives prospective parents second thoughts. The younger the child, the more likely persistent nagging is his or her technique. This type of nagging, which puts parents' backs up, isn't as effective as importance nagging.

Importance nagging requires some level of sophistication in manipula-tion. You will recognize importance nagging as "I have to have another book because I have already done everything in Volume 1 and you want me to learn don't you?" or "Where will my Hot Wheels sleep if they don't have the matching multi-level garage?" or "I'll be the only one in Grade Four without a Barbie pencil case ... how will I do my homework?"

Importance nagging usually appeals to the parents' desire to provide the best for their kids, an aspiration often associated with boomer parents. No one wants to see their kids left behind, so why not get the extras that will help them excel? Who wants the neighbourhood to think that they can't afford to get their son or daughter the latest bike? Parental ego goes a long way to help kids fuel their desire for "more." James McNeal calls these requests a "style" and says children use a variety of these styles to get what they want. In his book *Kids as Customers* he highlights these general appeals:

Educational	"You want me to learn, don't you?"
Health	"Don't you want me to be healthy?"
Time	"It will save you time."
Economy	"It will save you money."
Happiness	"You want me to be happy, don't you?"
Security	"You don't want me to get hurt, do you?"

Overall, importance nagging works better according to the Western International Media survey but persistence can still make a difference in some businesses. This "nag factor" research demonstrates that in the categories of food and beverages and movies, frequency and duration of the nag can pay off for kids.

Since the pestering of parents has been quantified it is not surprising that in the past marketing to children has predominantly been about creating the nag factor. Simply put, the idea has been that if you can make kids want it, you can get their parents to buy it. This tactic has fuelled business in cereal, snacks, and convenience and fast foods. The "hey kids" form of communication is likely responsible for many of those scenes you see played out every day in the aisles of grocery stores.

Some marketers also advertise to the parents to complement the pant-pulling technique. These parents are seen as "gatekeepers" and the goal is to soften them up so that they won't shut down the requests of the kids. In most kid food businesses today, the gatekeeper moms and dads are mostly extinct. One cereal marketer calls them "Mean

Moms." This reflects the child's attitude towards the gatekeeper role of the parent.

And while parents want to do what is best for their kids today, there is too little time and energy in their hectic lifestyles to deal with the battles of the no's. Parents pick their battles and the kids often get their crispy critters as a result. This influence can be seen in the increase in share of the pre-sweetened cereal market. It is one of the only segments (other than bran, but that is another demographic story) in the cereal category that has experienced continual growth over the 1990s. While Rice Krispies used to be the number-one choice for moms of toddlers, presweetened alternatives like Fruit Loops and Honey Nut Cheerios are now taking the top spots. Is this because moms think these cereals are better for their kids? No—anyone in the cereal business knows that moms still want nutritious cereals for their kids—but they also now know that moms believe nutrition sometimes means just getting their kids to eat. So when parents are short of time or patience or both, a pre-sweetened cereal is better than no breakfast at all. Kids rule when it comes to breakfast and the cereal companies know it.

Let's acknowledge that the economic impact of kids is worth paying attention to, but more interestingly, how does it happen?

We know there are a lot of factors at play: dual-income families have more money to spend; the pace of life is quickened to the point where purchases fill the gap for other emotional or sociological needs; and parents like to involve their kids in decision-making. As we've discussed earlier, there are many good reasons for including kids in decision-making today. But, we also wonder—is there a power struggle here? Do parents willingly oblige, or are they being manipulated by the demands of youth in their consuming frenzy? When the requests for stuff begin, is it the pushiness of kids or the weakness of the parents that puts kids in the decision-making seat? Some people, and they are usually older and of another generation, firmly believe that kids have a place and it is not in the adult world: "Imagine the ridiculousness of kids having a say in what I do as a parent! Not in our day. Kids knew their place." Others think that teens and tweens just think they have the power but really don't. "All kids think they rule and some adults just go along with that notion. When push comes to shove, kids are not in control." But when you ask the parents of the Generation Y what they have to say, you may be surprised by the answers.

FIGURE 3: *Perception of "Kidfluence" in Household Purchases*
The chart demonstrates that parents think kids have more influence than kids think they do.

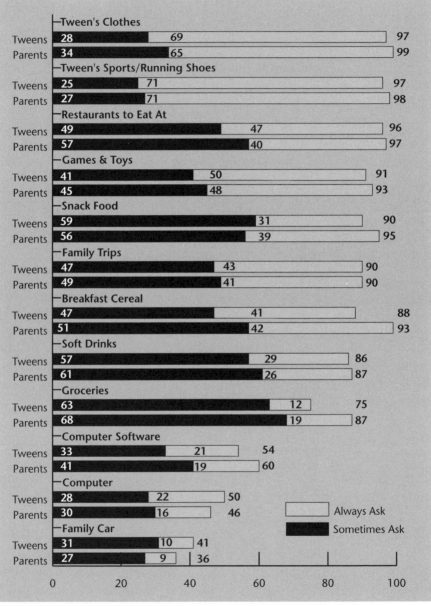

Source: *Creative Research International Inc.*

In the *YTV Kid & Tween Report*, parents claimed that their tweens have great influence on household purchases, more influence than the tweens themselves estimated (Figure 3). Parents say kids influence grocery purchases 83 per cent of the time, while tweens say they thought they influenced these purchases only 66 per cent of the time. And while we might expect consultation between parents and children on, say, kids clothes, it is interesting to note that parents also rely on the kids' input for family expenditures on trips, computers and cars.

So it may not be the kids pushing in, but the parents opening the door. A U.S. poll of parents done by Penn, Shoen & Berland Associates claims that kids influence 40 per cent of their parents' purchases, and that 65 per cent of parents explicitly solicit children's opinions about products used for the whole family. The NPD Group, a market research firm based in Port Washington, N.Y., published a study in 2000 which claimed that 71 per cent of the mothers polled said their kids' wishes are very influential. These 2,500 mothers with children under 10 believed that their children's influence was more important than advertising.

Kids' new power in family decision-making may be less about forceful kids and more about parents requesting input.

Once kids are let into the decision process they don't let up either. The U.S. poll showed that 42 per cent of them tell adults which brands to buy *all the time*. The YTV study shows some interesting differences in family

FIGURE 4: *Frequency of Telling Adults Which Brands to Buy*

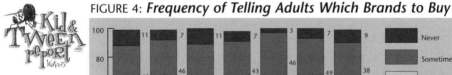

Source: YTV Kid & Tween Report, *1999.*

dynamics among the provinces in Canada. When you look at the numbers for Quebec and the rest of Canada you see that kids attempt to influence more in Quebec. 52 per cent of Quebec kids regularly tell adults what to buy, versus 44 per cent in the rest of Canada. One mother in Quebec feels that kids are generally more expressive of their opinions today, which might lead to more permission to speak their mind. "Kids today are confronted by what is in and out and they need to feel a part of it. They ask for what they want and they get it. Parents just want to please them and make them happy."

"Maybe kids today are spoiled," says one mother of two from Victoriaville who struggles with drawing the line. "We try not to give too much but you do get into the material thing. I want them to have what others have but I don't want to do too much. You have to stop yourself."

Pushovers or Meanies?

But it's not just the type of nagging that helps kids get things it also depends on the type of parent one is. And research confirms that true to our Quebec mom's point, unlike what most parents would want to admit publicly, the majority of parents (67 per cent) do give in to their kids' desires and demands.

According to the same Western International Media Corp. study on the nag factor there are four attitudinal types of parents:

Indulgers	33%
Bare Necessities	31%
Conflicted	20%
Kid Pals	15%

The numbers do not add up to 100 because of rounding.

Indulgers are the biggest segment of parents by a hair at 33 per cent, and are what most people would call "the pushover parents." It isn't surprising, given changing parenting styles and kidfluence, that this group is the largest. Indulgers are described as parents who spend impulsively and enjoy the possessions they acquire. Their average age is 35 and they have kids just up to their tween years. These are the parents who affect every other kid in the neighbourhood because the other parents will hear, "But Suzie has the newest [insert item here]—why can't I have one too?" These households are the most ethnically diverse and tend to be dual-income.

Bare Neccessities (31 per cent of parents) are the runner-up for largest attitudinal group, but they certainly do not represent the majority of parents. These parents are the oldest and most affluent of the segments and have total control of the spending in the household. They are frugal, consider carefully all purchases, and don't admit to kids influencing their brand choices. This group is most likely to have a computer at home and have low interaction with their children.

Conflicted parents are the next biggest segment at 20 per cent of parents, and they tend to be the parents who resent the requests for non-essentials but give in because they feel guilty. A large percentage of these households are headed by single parents. And where all working parents feel guilt sometimes and may compensate for it with some treats, the conflicted parent likely faces that situation far too often. This segment is the least affluent of all parents.

Kid pals at 15 per cent of parents just want to have fun with their kids and like to buy things they will enjoy as well. These parents are buying video games because they want to play it too, or taking the kids snow boarding and signing up for lessons themselves. They are the youngest of the parent groups and really enjoy the time they spend with their kids. Their kids are involved in many product and brand decisions in the household and Kid Pals believe that "advertising helps me choose products for my kids."

The "gimmes" are just part of having kids, as all parents know. The fact that pester power has been quantified for business analysis makes it easier for marketers to determine whether their business is impacted by this childish behaviour. Something for all businesses to consider is the statistic used by James McNeal, that when kids ask their parents for stuff, 90 per cent of their requests are for brand names. Another study supports this fact where researchers analyzed letters to Santa and discovered that kids expressed their wishes to Santa in brand names over 85 per cent of the time.

If these statistics hold true, the job of a marketer then becomes making his brand name highly recognizable and differentiating it in the

Are the Gimmes Getting to You?

If you are a parent concerned about increasing commercialism there are other parents like you. The Center for the New American Dream is a community on-line where the goal is to help families live better lives by minimizing the role of commercialization. They produced a brochure called *Tips for Parenting in a Commercial Culture*, which can be accessed at www.newdream.org. On the NewDream Web site you can participate in discussions, read articles and link to other related sites, like about.com which has a frugal living section.

kid's mind. Kids usually have one brand they prefer and one or two that are substitutes. Parents know which brands their kids prefer and usually won't buy outside of that short list when they are alone on shopping trips. Missing out on kids' preferences could mean losing a whole family's shopping.

Upping the Influence: From Penny Candy to Cars

Between asking for things they want and directly or indirectly stating their preferences on other household purchases, kids can rack up some mighty numbers. The automotive industry claims kidfluence impacted $17.7 billion in automobile purchases in 1997. One girls' clothing retailer estimates that girls aged 7 to 14 influence parental purchases worth $66 billion.

These figures are mindboggling. *Billions?* From kids bugging their parents? Admittedly these numbers are all guesstimates because "influence" is difficult to accurately quantify. The wild variations reported in a variety of articles and studies arise from authors using different age brackets and including different purchases to capture their estimation of the total financial impact.

The billions that kids influence goes well beyond pester power. The kidfluence is the result of kids being actively involved in family purchase decisions. Today kids get a vote in family discussions regarding both major and minor purchases because of the trend in child-rearing to a more consultative or shared-power philosophy.

This type of influence is not a new phenomenon. As early as 1948, advertising trade journals referred to children exerting tremendous influence in the selection and purchase of televisions. What is new are the numbers attached to kidfluence. In the 1960s it is estimated that kids influenced $5 billion of parental purchases. By the 1970s the figure had grown to $20 billion and to by 1984 it was $50 billion. In 1990 it was $132 billion; and the latest estimate, for 1997, was $188 billion. Kidfluence today means very big business.

Three decades and 170-odd billion dollars later. The increase in dollars is beyond the trend of kids influencing. These numbers also reflect the increase in new kid-directed products that are for sale today. The total number of product categories that kids participate in has expanded to include high-ticket items like computers, travel and cars.

Car manufacturers may have been the first to react to this influence when the minivans hit the market. These rolling family rooms allowed families to spend more time on the road and travel together in greater comfort and this created a demand for new conveniences. When one minivan brand figured out that the right placement of cup holders and backseat audio jacks could sway the kids, and thus affect the parents' decision on what van to buy, they made changes to the interior designs and advertised the changes. To show how much they think of kids in their overall approach, Ford started using cartoons in their minivan ads. While they may suggest that the cartoons were merely an unusual way to reach adults, an observer could also conclude that it was an attempt to grab the attention of the younger viewers and perhaps form a brand attachment or at least a brand awareness. This seems more likely the case when Ford followed up the television campaign with a Ford Fairy Tale colouring book that was sent to subscribers of *Today's Parent* magazine. In it kids can colour around cartoon figures and selling features like *Power Adjustable Pedals* and the *Reverse Sensing System*. Was it the colouring kids or the supervising parents that Ford was trying to reach with this message?

GM is going one step beyond advertising with cartoons, with the launch of the Chevrolet Venture Warner Bros. Edition minivan with a built-in television and Bugs Bunny nameplates. In the launch news coverage, the reporter in the *Toronto Star* opened the article with the comment, "For any parent of a child under 10, this is a warning: If you are shopping for a new vehicle, do not let your kids see this one, or you will end up driving it home." This reporter is headlining the impact of kidfluence in the car business. GM is building grassroots events around this launch in which the Warner Bros. characters can mingle with their public and GM can make the outing to a car dealership a family fun event.

General Motors believes kids are an important secondary market because kids shop with their parents and are powerful influencers. In this case the influence doesn't come from the gimmes but from the fact that their kids are a prime consideration when parents are choosing a car. They want their families to be safe and comfortable and they want the car to fit their functional needs on a daily basis. GM uses the example of the fourth door on the Chevy Venture as an example of kids being a secondary consumer. Even though kids didn't directly ask for it, the door was designed to appeal to both parents and kids to increase comfort and loading convenience and any family that has a van with the fourth door knows what a big advantage it is.

GM invites kids to car clinics and concept-car introductions to get their input on design and assess their overall interest. GM also has a task force to get at what will appeal to the Generation Y audience to ensure their brand is in the running when these kids become car buyers themselves.

Influencing purchases is just one type of kid vote in the family. Kids also express their opinions on what family vacation to take, what schools they attend and what kind of birthday party they have. Boomers believe participating in this sort of family dialogue helps their children prepare for the real world. In the example of the family vacation, some new and surprising businesses are emerging due to kidfluence.

Influence has Changed the Travel Business

When one thinks of cruises one tends to think of the senior set playing shuffleboard on deck or honeymooners in exotic ports of call, but the cruise business today is all about family fun. At the end of the 1990s Disney launched two new ships to expand their share of the family vacation dollar, and Premier Cruise Lines' Big Red Boat entertains kids with Looney Tunes characters and offers large, family-size cabins. The Carnival Cruise Line "Fun Ship" isn't just for adult swingers any more; now they have Camp Carnival for kids 2–17 and 24-hour pizzerias. Carnival Cruises have had 250,000 kids on their ships in part due to their programs like Homework Helper that encourage families to cruise even during the school season. Industry statistics show that cruises to date have hosted 700,000 kids on board and they expect this number to grow.

More families today travel and enjoy holidays at resorts and in hotels. More and more school-aged kids are seasoned flyers, taking exciting trips to places like Disney World. The boomers want to continue to have new experiences and travel is one way of sharing the world and time with their kids. Years ago travel was seen as an indulgence, but today it is considered more of a life education and as necessary family downtime in a pressure-cooker world for two working parents. According to Kate Pocock, senior editor of *Travel & More* magazine, the travel world is being redefined by families vacationing together. "There's been a gradual shift in the last five years. And it is not just travel companies jumping on the bandwagon. Resorts and cruises also have a lot more kids' programs because families are travelling more with kids."

The reality of two working parents has also changed vacation time. Hotels are starting to realize that they can attract conference and meeting business from the business travellers by offering something for their kids. One hotel manager claims meeting planners mention right away that there has to be something for the participants' kids. "If we didn't have good programs for the kids we would lose the business." At the Ritz Carlton in Boston, the "Ritz Kids" program entertains kids day and night while parents are at meetings. "We are seeing evidence of just how important time-deprived parents are and just how important it is for them to incorporate business and pleasure," states a Ritz manager in an article from the *New York Times Magazine*. And while this may not be the average North American's situation, it does demonstrate the power of kidfluence reaching even into niche segments.

"Kidtailing" to Generation Y

The influence of kids is felt in many ways and in many places. "Kidtailing" is a new term used by *USA Today* writer Bruce Horovitz in his article about a wide range of retailers who have made it their goal to encourage the whole family to shop. Home Depot has workshops for kids, Starbucks is testing a play area, and U.S. bookseller Barnes and Noble offers weekly reading and craft sessions. Retailers have discovered that if they get the families to stay longer, they spend more. Store sales during a kid promotion for one retailer jumped as much as 30 per cent, and Home Depot sees an increase in daily sales when they host kid workshops. Over three million kids in the United States have participated over the two years since the Home Depot program was introduced, and the retailer is counting on those three million customers for life. Beyond workshops and promotions for kids, play areas are of real interest to parents—they get to shop in peace while their kids are having fun—and everyone from grocery stores to IKEA to sit-down restaurants are offering up diversions for the kids. A survey by Burger King found that nine out of 10 parents would return to Burger King again so that their kids could play at the Fun Centers.

Recognizing the value of kidfluence means linking your company with the new up-and-coming generation of adults.

Kidfluence can happen when kids are secondary consumers or influencers in many purchase situations. The considerable force of the direct and indirect influences of kids create economic implications too great to ignore. When businesses today struggle to find new growth and differentiation in this ultra-competitive world, kids may be an unidentified or undervalued opportunity.

As one business person put it, this is not about marketing kidstuff: this is about attaching yourself to a generation coming of age.

SPEED READ SUMMARY

- The influence market impacts business far beyond any traditional notion of a "kid business."
- Kids exert their influence by asking their parents to buy things for them. Parents say a child's appeal to them has more influence on their shopping than advertising does. And Generation Y kids also vote on family purchases because they want to and because their parents ask them to.
- Parents feel kids have more influence than the kids themselves estimate.

- Kids can be direct, indirect or secondary influencers of a purchase.
- The impact of kidfluence is huge and growing. Businesses need to know how kids fit into their market if they want the family's business.
- Kidfluence is felt in unexpected places (such as phone providers) and with big-ticket family purchases (cars and travel).
- Kids are not a niche target but a generation coming of age.

10

Kids as Future Purchasers

Man creates culture and
through culture creates himself.
—*Pope John Paul II*

The future market of kids is the toughest one to understand from an economic point of view because it is not quantifiable. We cannot predict how much kids will spend as adults given the many outside influences that would come into play in such an equation. But lifetime value is an important concept in managing businesses today and one worth investigating.

Lifetime value is a relatively new term outside of direct one-to-one and relationship marketing that explains what a customer is worth to a business over a long period of time. Some companies track one-time sales of individual products and other companies track the relationship with the customer who is buying and possibly rebuying the same or additional products from one company. A lifetime value equation is especially important to companies such as telecommunications that can sell many services to one customer. For example, if you are a Rogers AT&T customer, your lifetime value to the company is the amount you pay for basic cable, your cellphone and your video rentals, if you purchase all three from Rogers AT&T. Relationship marketers believe smart companies manage these customer relationships so they can maximize and protect revenue with each customer. It is less expensive to keep customers than to attract new customers. The challenge for a business is to recognize when new customers enter their markets and how early a new relationship can be forged. Developing a brand relationship with kids may be the way to develop fresh new customers on an ongoing basis.

But when we think of kids as future customers we are also dealing with the issue of marketing to kids. Some companies and individuals are uncomfortable with the notion of marketing to kids. Some see kid marketing as manipulation or commercial assault on the unprotected. Some think that advertising to kids shouldn't be allowed. A highly regarded creative advertising professional in Canada refuses to work on assignments that target kids due to his strong beliefs. Chris Staples is a founding partner of the communications company Rethink in Vancouver. Prior to launching Rethink in 1999 he was the most celebrated creative director in Canada for many years, while working at Palmer Jarvis Advertising. His creative leadership in advertising is legendary and he has some strong points of view on marketing to children, which he shared with us in his own words:

> The conventional wisdom is this generation (Generation Y) is somehow more marketing savvy than any other in history. I wonder if this is just wishful thinking on the part of guilty adults (especially those in media and marketing). It is clear that marketing and advertising messages are far more pervasive today than they were in the 60's and 70's. Five-year-old girls singing along with Britney Spears. Bedtime stories with the inevitable video, doll and collectible stickers. My eight-year-old niece wears makeup.
>
> But just because today's kids look sophisticated doesn't mean they actually are sophisticated. In fact, I think they're less able than previous generations to distinguish between what's real and true, and what's calculated and manufactured. Who can blame them? Even adults have a tough time deciding if a magazine cover story is real or a P.R. puff piece, trying to sell a movie, a CD, a clothing line.

Gail Golden, a psychologist and professor at University of Western Ontario, says that research shows that children are more suggestible than adults: "Kids don't have the same cognitive abilities so they are particularily vulnerable. They tend to swallow things whole." But she also adds that because we live in a free-market capitalist society she cannot justify banning advertising to children. "It's up to the adults in kids' lives to teach them to take ads with a grain of salt."

Whether they choose to advertise to kids or not, companies need to recognize that kids are future customers and their childhood memories will influence them as buying adults. A business can look at kids as the future market, and consider them an investment in their brand equity, regardless of whether they are presently an advertising target, and consider what role kids can or should play in their business plans.

If a child doesn't know or like a brand, will they be less likely to buy it as an adult? No one can really answer that question, but most brand managers can tell a story about a brand loyalist who grew up using the brand they love now as adults, or how they watched a parent or friend use the brand. So we can't quantify the impact of kids as consuming adults but we can predict that global brands will still want to be in business in the next 10 to 20 years. And **Brand loyalty can last a lifetime.** we do know that brand loyalty is the equity on which these companies are valued and survive. So it could be argued that kids' preferences today do matter—as a deposit in the brand bank of goodwill.

How can one determine the value of a kid/tween/teen preferring the taste of Coke or liking the fit of Gap jeans? Will a little boy who played with toy Porsches grow up with a fervent desire for a real one? Will a mom serve her child Cheerios because she liked them best when she was young? These are the questions on many marketers' minds when they are building brand loyalty. The concept of brand loyalty is more about affecting the behaviour of the future than it is about rewarding today's purchases. Allegiance to a particular brand can last a lifetime. Many women use what their mothers used to wash the dishes or the family clothes. Many women wear the same makeup they did when they were teens, or use the same feminine hygiene products.

Loyalty has become a big buzzword in the last few years given the increasing need to be competitive and the growing interest in one-to-one marketing due to the fragmentation of mass media. Kids seem to be an overlooked opportunity in the consideration of the loyalty effect.

When you peruse the hundreds of business books written on the subject of brand and customer loyalty, the opportunity of growing up with your customers isn't covered. The content in all of these books is focused on retaining the current customer (an adult) and maximizing his or her lifetime value to the company. But how did that adult become a current customer that was worth retaining? Did his early experiences with a brand impact the choices he made as an adult? Did she go from being a tween or teen using a product to a young adult or mother choosing the same brand? Imagine if the lifetime value of the customer was calculated from the age of 12 or eight or even six. What would the financial impact be? What if every child represented thousands of dollars in lifetime value versus hundreds from when they become adults? Would that change a company's business model?

The financial viability of considering kids an important market segment and investing in them today depends on the type of business. Some businesses work on such tight financial scenarios, with a quarter to quarter focus, that long-term investments are not considered viable. But a case could be made given what we know about brand development and behaviour influences to not overlook kids as important business influences.

Many kid marketing experts would agree that not paying attention to kids today is missing a key ingredient for long-term success. In Dan S. Acuff's book *What Kids Buy and Why* he states that in his experience many categories lend themselves to early brand identification. He adds that "at YMS [Youth Marketing Systems, a research and consulting company] we have often marvelled at the fact that more adult targeting companies, such as automobile companies, gasoline companies and beverage companies, don't address these early brand identification patterns by targeting younger audiences."

Lynne DeCew, managing director of Vancouver's Kid Think, a kid specialty division of advertising agency DDB, believes brand loyalty is developed in childhood and that it can last a lifetime. "If you think of them as kids or teens, a special target group, you fail to see them as the consumers they are becoming." But she understands that some businesses have difficulty thinking about the impact of kids because it is hard to invest in something when it won't pay off for a long time.

One industry that is looking at kids for the long term is banks. Bank accounts for kids may not pay dividends for years, but some banks believe that when a kid opens an account he or she is likely to keep it for life, and that makes the child a valuable business target. "Kids are most likely to open an account where their parents bank," says DeCew, so she recommends banks talk to both parents and kids. "CIBC has books targeted to parents that talk about educating kids on money and saving." The mutual fund industry is also interested in parents and kids. Trimark developed an RESP program that educated parents on what the future holds for their kids, and Aim Financial took it one step further and offered a CD-ROM called *Henry the Hedgehog's Big Adventure* in their RESP package. Appealing to both the kid and the parent is beneficial not only today but tomorrow, according to a senior financial services manager. "We are in the business of lifetime relationships. Children are an important part of our clients' lives and whatever the bank does to assist their children not only builds a relationship with the child but also with the parent."

Creating Cross-Generation Appeal
Some companies have experienced real success by winning both the parents and kids. The recent successes of the iMac launch and the VW Beetle relaunch demonstrate the power of appealing across generations.

The new Beetle's launch advertising used overt links to the brand memories and attachments of a previous generation while it was attracting a new, younger clientele. The car is loved and driven by the boom, and generations X and the older Ys. The true strength of the brand was apparent in the wide-ranging success of the new Beetle. A new generation will now grow up with the Beetle and it will form their opinions and preferences for the Volkswagen brand. VW states that overall Volkswagen sales lifted with the relaunch of the Beetle, an effect they believe comes from attributing the positive values of one car across their whole line. How many kids will now drive Beetles or Jettas or Passats when they are ready to own their own cars due to the nostalgia felt for the Bug?

The iMac is another product that transcends generations. The computer industry was stunned by the iMac success and its appeal to first-time computer buyers. Apple found a way to re-energize the computer industry by adding colour and design to its user-friendly Macintosh brand. Kids today will now demand other computer and technology companies to be as cool and accessible as iMac. You can already see the influence the iMac has had on other technology products, such as coloured printers and zip drives. Whether these were intentional moves for Volkswagen and Apple is unknown, but no one can argue with the impact their products have made and the brand status that has come from the popularity with parents and their kids. Apple has to be happy with bringing in a new wave of computer users because their first experiences may form a lifetime bond that the company will benefit from for years to come.

A big part of the appeal of both of these examples was in the stylishness of the product. Kool-Aid, a powdered drink mix made by Kraft Canada, also wanted to appeal to two generations but didn't have inherent style going for it, so the marketing and advertising group had to generate interest with a created "cool" image. "Be Kool" was the call to action seen on outdoor boards around the country in Canada in the late 1990s. It was an invitation to both moms and kids to buy and drink the perennial favourite Kool-Aid drink mix. Kool-Aid wanted to reach the mom who was buying and the kids who would be drinking and asking for their preferred drinks. "Hitting a dual target can be a real challenge," says John Farquhar, Creative Director of Young and Rubicam in 1999, the advertising agency responsible for the Kraft Canada campaign. "The trick is to make sure you are not too focused on one target or the other. Luckily, Kool-Aid is a power brand that consumers of all ages are familiar with." The campaign took the nostalgic Kool-Aid jug character that moms would have grown up with and brought that equity to a new generation with large bright happy faces, some imprinted on iconic summer images like the bottom of a swimming pool and a green leaf. The advertising campaign was so successful (a sure sign when people were stealing the posters out of subway stations) that it continued to run for several years. Kids liked the bright faces and moms fondly remembered their own childhoods and Kraft Canada made kidfluence work for them all summer long.

Brand equity can develop in many ways—both with and without marketing or advertising directly to kids. But some companies make it a mission to reach kids today to overtly develop that lifetime bond and relationship. In the car industry the pay off for advertising to kids may be 15 years down the road, but GM is one company that thinks the investment is worth it. Phil Guarascio, VP General Manager of North American Operations in 1999, spoke at the Retailing to Kids and Teens conference that year and stated that GM spends 10 per cent of their advertising budget on programs targeted at kids. When asked why they market to people who can't buy cars, he responded that kids know at the age of 10 what cars they want to buy. The focus of GM's marketing effort is to create qualified traffic for the dealerships. Guarascio believes that traffic starts when kids form their impressions of cars and certain types of cars. Because kids love speed and extreme things, they naturally love cars. By tapping into that inherent emotional interest a brand relationship can be developed at an early age, and that in turn translates into future qualified traffic at a car dealership.

In Canada, Ford's interest in kids goes beyond marketing and branding. Rob Hodge, the Advertising Manager at Ford Canada, says Ford has always been interested in youth but that now they are embracing a youthful mindset.

"Youth is much more than a demographic. At Ford we are deep diving to determine the 'youth state of mind' and expanding that into the Ford culture. The youth mindset has appeal, and is aspirational to the population at large while also being important because they are over 20 per cent of the population." Beyond seeking young people's input into their efforts, Ford is bringing youth into their planning process. "We have a saying 'For youth, by youth' which may be a corny turn of phrase but it is true. By bringing kids into the process earlier we benefit from their direct feedback and unfiltered ideas. Rather than guessing what they would like in a car and researching it after the fact, we work with them to build it. By approaching our work this way we end up with better product as an end result." Ford has worked with many experts to help them understand the "whole youth mindset." The NRG group of Toronto and Ford's agency Young and Rubicam are instrumental in developing programs and unique approaches to get Ford closer to the pulse of youth. When asked if he thought that his interest in youth may be a passing thing due to current demographic trends, Hodge stated a belief that his team will always think youth is important. "We are searching for the underlying core attributes of youth as a culture and cultural things change over time. We will need to continually tap into where they are and, more importantly, where they are going."

Ford believes in kidfluence because they know that attachment to vehicles starts at a young age. "It's an emotional issue. Car branding indirectly happens at every stage of life. Kids' impressions of a car make and model begin when they are introduced to the car. Ford's goal is to be there at every stage of the consumer's life. The earlier, the better."

The Branding Age

So if kids are important to the long-term health of a brand or business segment, and a company wants to develop a relationship, how do companies know when it is the right time to reach them? *Is* there a right time or optimum time to develop future customers? As we all know, kids consume and kids want things. But when do they become brand consumers? If 90 per cent of all requests from children are made with brand names, one wonders if there is a specific age when branding occurs.

Both academic and media-based research shows that kids are aware of brands from a very early age. But if you're a parent, you don't need research to confirm that; there's plenty of anecdotal evidence: "I couldn't believe it when Rachel asked to watch *Teletubbies* and then wanted Tinkie Winkie for Christmas. She's only two."

Kids know brands today. "At 20 months kids will start to recognize some of the thousands of brands they see every day," according to Kealy Wilkinson, former director of The Alliance for Children and Television. "Kids are now exposed to marketing earlier and earlier. The Teletubbies are pitched at kids who are preverbal. And it [the show] is successful because of the sales of the toys."

Much research has been done on the impact of TV and advertising to children and one source indicates that kids between the ages of two and five and pay a lot of attention to commercials. Because of that, they become aware of many products and services. It has been determined though, that kids at this age don't know the difference between an advertisement and the program, so while they are aware of products they don't necessarily recognize an ad as a sales pitch or become persuaded by it.

Kids also have their older siblings to introduce them to brands. A three-year-old will know McDonald's, but this knowledge could be a result of having older siblings and a few Happy Meals under his belt rather than because of a TV commercial. And with kids shopping with their parents so much today they are exposed in stores and malls to thousands of products and brands.

It would be difficult to determine where kids learn most about brands—through TV, siblings, at school, in the park, or out shopping—but James McNeal claims that kids have a brand repertoire of 100 brands by the time they enter grade one. By the age of 10 this increases to 300–400 brands and as adults we carry over 1,500 brands in our repertoire. A brand repertoire is not which brands one is aware of but the list of brands that one chooses from, or their favourites in each category. For example someone could have a brand repertoire of three chocolate bars that includes their favourite Mr. Big and second and third favourites Mars and Smarties that are sometimes substituted for a Mr. Big.

A brand repertoire is usually developed by trying different products and brands. This is a function of choice more than it is influence from a mass medium. The size of these repertoires are indicative of the consumer culture we live in. We have many chocolate bars from which to choose. Walking the aisles in any store one can see the dizzying array of choices we have as consumers.

Brands are everywhere in our culture today, so kids of all ages will be exposed at every turn and with that comes the power of recognition or awareness. But awareness is only one step in brand identification. A younger child may be able to demand what they know or see, but when does a kid know that one brand is better than another brand? A toddler wants blue juice, a kindergarten child wants to wear dresses to school, a four-year-old demands fruit-coloured loops in the cereal aisle. In each of these cases the item is more important than the actual brand. It is the immediacy of seeing and wanting that creates so much of the pester power parents experience. But the power of a brand is in its ability to provide differentiation for the consumer. James McNeal believes kids as young as three and four do have brand preferences. His theory is that kids believe the brands they use are better due to the egocentric nature of kids: "I use it therefore it is better." This preference he believes is the formation of brand loyalty.

But one could argue that until the brand has meaning to its consumer, it is not a brand. A brand is a promise of performance that is recognized and trustworthy. Brands have distinguishing characteristics that live in the hearts and minds of consumers. So if a four-year-old claims to prefer a brand but doesn't equate the liking of the product to a higher brand value like popularity, leadership or personal identification, it is most likely a taste, colour or look preference more than a discerning brand choice. At the young ages of four and five products are likely meeting more basic, immediate needs. The way McNeal describes preference is not necessarily differentiation. And preference does not necessarily equate to meaning.

To differentiate one needs the ability to discern and relate. To differentiate and choose one must have the cognitive ability. Interestingly, the stages of child development suggest that children younger than the age of seven are unlikely to relate on this level because they have not yet developed that part of their brain.

To understand this we look to Jean Piaget, the Swiss biologist who in the 1900s pioneered the most comprehensive account of cognitive development in children, with his unique scientific approach integrating biology, psychology and epistemology. Reviewing his work we learn that Piaget believed that kids progress through a series of stages in their thinking, from sensori-motor to pre-operational to concrete operational to formal operational. Each growth stage focuses on different areas of cognitive development (see Figure 1).

From birth to the age of five the brain is creating its structure of knowledge, its "hardwiring," or the brain's "world view," by processing brain patterns from sensory experience. Kids progress through the sensori-motor stage when they learn by doing. Child development specialists have observed that kids begin doing with intent. Intent precedes the ability. A child grasps for an object long before they have the ability to hold it. The brain is developing and being stimulated by the environment and the child learns by practising and exploring. Joseph Chilton Pearce, who authored a book, *Magical Child*, on the development of the human brain, says that "from birth, the growth of intelligence is a progression from the concrete toward the abstract. The greater the structure that is built, the greater the ability to interact with more content."

A child normally has acquired 80 per cent of his or her concrete knowledge at about three years of age. The rest of the world view takes seven years to develop. Many stages of social and emotional development occur during the toddler and early school years but the brain doesn't move into another physical growth spurt until the age of seven. The physical change comes when the two hemispheres of the brain, the right and left, begin to specialize.

FIGURE 1 *Jean Piaget's Theory of Cognitive Development*

Age	Stage
0–2	**Sensori-Motor** Children are involved in active exploration of the world and are obtaining a basic knowledge of objects via their five senses.
2–7	**Pre-operational** Children can develop language and can use symbols. They engage in elementary reasoning such as the ability to classify and count. They experience the fearful in the world and deal with it through dreams, play and attachments to symbols (eg. a teddy bear).
7–12	**Concrete Operational** Children begin to think logically and organize their knowledge. They can manipulate symbols leading to the ability to read and work with numbers. Rules help them organize their thoughts (eg. grammar) and their world (eg. game rules).
12+	**Formal Operational** Children can reason realistically and deal with abstractions. They can manipulate second order abstractions (eg. algebra) in which letters stand for numbers, which stand for objects. They are able to construct theories thereby helping them form an identity.

There is a significant shift at this age from right brain to left brain development. The left brain is involved in the development of the ability of intellect, logic and reasoning. This shift moves the child from black-and-white thinking to moral thinking, and from primarily fantasy play to more reality play. This shift also begins to take the child from childish unawareness to assessing and observing the world around him or her. This is the stage Piaget refers to as the concrete operational stage. From seven to the age of 12 kids begin to develop and understand their personal power in the world. This personal power is a result of developing autonomy, from becoming physically independent of parental help and the active period of neurological changes which develop more adult thinking patterns.

In advertising surveys we see the two hemispheres of the brain in action when seven- to nine-year-olds year olds can differentiate between programming and advertising and know that the advertising is trying to persuade them, whereas younger kids between three and five cannot distinguish the TV programming from the advertising.

Ernst Hilgard of Stanford University, quoted in *Magical Child*, claims kids become highly susceptible to suggestion at the age of seven. Kids at this age can begin to construct concepts but they are still linked to action or the concrete world. For an example of the link between the concrete and conceptual worlds of seven-year-olds, the book tells the story of the Israeli entertainer in the 1970s named Geller who could bend metal without touching it. He was performing his act on TV in England when as an experiment he asked the audience to join him and try to bend metal while watching. Some 1,500 reports were called into the BBC, and upon further investigation it was discovered that the vast majority of people who claimed they bent metal while watching the show were kids aged seven to 14. This experiment was repeated in many countries over the next year with the same results. They found the average age of spoon benders was nine. Chilton Pearce, the author who shared this story, believes that TV had a role in this experiment, given that TV is such a powerful influencer of suggestion. He also believes that the nine-year-old's world view is not completely hardened and that because kids at this stage are open to suggestion, have the necessary logic to deal with abstract concepts and can operate on concrete suggestions, the combination makes them more susceptible to the metal-bending experiment. If so, could it be true that the nine- year-old brain is open enough for brands to create lifelong impressions?

Tweens and Brands

Not a little kid any more and almost a teen, tweens are definitely brand aware and possibly forming lifetime connections and preferences. The moment of "branding impact" appears to be at this crucial point, given everything that is happening in their intellectual and social development.

Psychologists have called the ages between eight to 12 the years of rules and roles. Kids are forming their views of the world and defining where they fit in. They are looking for role models to help guide them and they want to conform so they fit in with their desired peer group. Younger kids are in need of their parents to do many things and be everything for them. At eight a child begins to look outside of his family for information, socializing and context. It doesn't mean the family doesn't matter, just that its primary importance has changed. Friends are paramount. In her book *The Nurture Assumption* Judith Harris puts forth an argument that peers matter more than parents when it comes to the social development of kids. As kids mature and become tweens, they have one foot in childhood and one in the adult world. This group may be impressionable but they have most of the thinking and perception tools of an adult, according to the observations of Jean Piaget. Most kids have adult thinking capacity by the age of 15. The only remaining adult tools that have yet to be developed at this age are advanced abstract thinking, including self-reflection.

Tweens are processing information like adults while being exposed to marketing at their schools, in their communities, and through every mass media contact. They are making important connections to products and brands based on their need to fit in and gain approval. This is prime brand imprinting territory.

These little adults are now making choices. The left brain provides the ability to discern. An eight-year-old can now appreciate the differences between products. It's not just a pair of jeans, as it is to a five-year-old; now it is low riding jeans with four pockets and stitching on the hem. These details are important when a tween is experimenting with self-expression.

The need for reality pushes tweens away from the fantasy life of their younger years. They want to associate themselves with an older world linked to an adult's reality. Barbie makes this transition because Barbie offers a young girl a teen lifestyle. This doesn't mean that fantasy is not part of tweens' lives but the emphasis changes in how they play and the entertainment they choose. The movie *Titanic* gave tween girls an adult fantasy and they in response made it the number-one-selling movie of all time around the world. Brands are a link to the real world. Brands help tweens emulate real role models.

Tweens are group-oriented because they look outside themselves for an identity and acceptance. They are concerned with what their peers think of them. They need to know what their peers value, and prefer to determine where they fit in. They are conformists because they will like what their friends like. This peer pressure can determine the clothes they wear, and the music they listen to. According to Janet Morrison, a psychological associate in Toronto, conforming is more important to tweens than younger children. "They are vulnerable to 'in' and 'out' clothes. They want to fit in, not be unique. They want to be physically like their friends." Morrison adds that "kids' judgements can be harsh at this age."

Tweens need to identify with a role model. This desire to relate to a group and be accepted drives their interest in many sports figures, celebrities and musicians. Nike's rise to power was in direct proportion to the rise of the youth market's hero Michael Jordan. Industry watchers now are wondering whether Nike can remain strong with this generation since Jordan retired.

Brands offer a promise of an identity and lifestyle and that's what tweens are looking for—an identity. Tweens can discern the differences between brands and understand why they are choosing one over another. As we've discussed, at younger ages, the brand doesn't play as strong a role as the basic product. The tween wants something more. An eight-year-old knows that a brand is different from a product because it matters that his friends choose the same brand. An eight-year-old knows that a brand is deemed cool or hot in comparison to other products, and that makes it more desirable. The school environment plays a big role in the development of the need for brands. Kids at home at younger ages don't have the social comparisons that school-aged kids have. Kids see their best friends with a certain look or item and they want to adopt the same look. Brands are badges that help people belong, and kids want and need to belong.

Deborah Roedder John described this time as the "analytical stage" in the development of becoming a consumer. Quite different from cognitive development this research looks at consuming habits of kids. Roedder John wrote a report called "Consumer Socialization of Children: A Retrospective Look at 25 years of Research," which was published by the *Journal of Consumer Research*, University of Chicago Press, in 1999. In her report she talks of there being three stages of consumer development with kids. The Perceptual Stage (ages three to seven) is where kids are aware of products but don't differentiate brands. The Analytical Stage (ages eight to 11) when brand awareness begins, and the Reflective Stage (ages 12–16) when adolescents are highly sensitive to brands and start to become sceptical.

Further evidence on how brands fit into tween lives can be found in the book *Creating Ever Cool*. Author Gene Del Vecchio shared a chart titled "Fear and Anxieties" (see Figure 2) to demonstrate how kids' fears change over time. The kids aged six to nine list social rejection, criticism and new situations as their top fears. Given these fears one can understand why brands start to play an important role in a kid's life. The right clothes, the right toys and hobbies will help them gain acceptance and approval by their peers. When kids are younger they are more focused on their safety within the family, but school-aged kids start to look beyond the family for social interaction and need outside reassurance on who they are.

The Roper Youth Report is another study that shows how things change at the age of eight or when becoming a tween. Their research shows how kids progress from purchasing things with parents to making independent

FIGURE 2: **What Kids Fear at Different Ages**

0–5	6–9	10–12	13–16
Separation	Social rejection	Kidnapping	Sexual relations
Loss of parent	Criticism	Divorce	Drug use
Divorce	New situations	Personal danger	Crowds
Noises	Burglars	War	Gossip
Animals	Injury	Alone in the dark	Kidnapping
Monsters	Divorce		Terrorism
	Personal danger		Divorce
	War		Personal danger
	Animals		War
	Monsters		

Source: Creating Ever-Cool: A Marketer's Guide to a Kid's Heart *by Gene Del Vecchio © 1997. Used by permission of the licenser, Pelican Publishing Company, Inc.*

choices. The question in the study asks, "What items do you pick out for yourself without needing to ask a parent before choosing?" The study indicates that the ages between eight and 13 are a turning point for how much a parent is involved in a purchase, regardless of who is paying (see Figure 3).

FIGURE 3: *Tweens Start Choosing Products on Their Own*

Here is a list of products. Please read down the list and for each one tell me if it is something you *usually* pick out for yourself without needing to ask a parent about before choosing, or is it something you usually need to check with a parent before choosing, or if it is something your parent chooses for you, or do you never buy it?

	6–7		8–12		13–17	
	Boys %	**Girls** %	**Boys** %	**Girls** %	**Boys** %	**Girls** %
Candy or snacks	36	39				
Soft drinks	36	28				
Food from fast food places	31	37	61	53	87	89
Books	19	30	50	50	68	82
Games or toys	19	29	50	39	76	69
Clothes	NA	NA	30	23	71	70
Athletic shoes or sneakers	NA	NA	28	25	68	69
Compact disc or tapes	4	9	34	26	75	81
Magazines	11	12	32	29	70	79
Jewelry	NA	NA	14	31	40	70
Video games	13	11	33	17	66	49
Video movie rentals	11	14	24	16	64	60
Personal care products	NA	NA	11	15	45	59
Video movies you buy	NA	NA	16	10	53	49
Computer software/ CD-ROMs	1	—	7	3	25	20

Source: *1996* Roper Youth Report. Copyright © 1996 Roper Starch Worldwide, Inc., 205 East 42nd Street, New York, NY 10017.

In the soft drinks category, only 36 per cent of kids who are six can choose a soft drink by themselves. But by the age of eight, 73 per cent of kids make the choice independently and the percentage increases again at the age of 13, to 92 per cent. This holds true with fast food as well. Imagine the impact of the decision of which brand to buy first—Coke or Pepsi? If you had this information as the marketing head of a soft drink company, would you consider six-year-olds, eight-year-olds, or 20-year-olds as your brand prospect?

The big shift when girls choose their purchases by themselves is with clothes and music. At the age of eight, 23 per cent of girls pick clothing without a parent, but this rises to 70 per cent by the age of 13. At the age of eight, 26 per cent of girls pick CDs or tapes, a percentage that increases to 81 per cent who choose independently at the age of 13.

More proof of the strength of the tween consumer is found in James McNeal's con-sumer development study. His study shows that while some kids buy at ages as young as five, for most kids independent purchases happen around the age of eight. His findings claim that this holds true regardless of income, education or number of children in the family. The only factor that impacts the age of independent purchasing is single-parent households. Kids who likely play a larger role in family purchasing overall start buying alone as young as seven.

The tween years are important years for many reasons. The brain's biggest growth spurt draws to a close around the age of 10. Tweens' brains are intellectually developing and operating closer to adults. Kids are socially developing beyond their families into the broader community. And all hell is breaking loose hormonally. And on top of that they are shopping with a lot of money in their pockets. The consuming experiences at this stage may represent a lifetime of buying behaviour. The brands that connect with tweens may benefit for many years to come.

Stay Young Forever

The future of brands doesn't always start as early as eight.

In some businesses just staying young is important. The lesson of some brand marketers today is that keeping your eye on the kids as they become teens and then young adults is crucial to long-term survival. Two high-profile cases are Levi's and Toyota.

> "Skiing is old-fashioned, elitist and boring—
> something that your parents do."
>
> —*according to a Teenage Snowboarder in the Economist*

When kids say this, business beware. What happens when a brand is rejected by the next generation? Consider the stock price of Levi Strauss and Co. By now everyone has discussed the demise of the great brand Levi's. The story goes that Levi's depended on its success with the boomers for both their jean business and new casual clothing businesses and ignored the role of the future market for their core denim business. By the time Levi's noticed they had stumbled from a 30 per cent share of the jean market to below 20 per cent they had to scramble to get in touch with the younger audience.

This mighty brand lost touch with kids. "We got older and we lost touch with teenagers," says David Spangler, director of market research. Levi's weren't cool any more—actually it was worse than that—they were "your dad's jeans." The Cool Monitor by Environics, a national polling company, showed kids described Levi's as worn by someone who lived in the country, was friendly and boring, drove a Cavalier or pickup and was really old. Any of these descriptors is the kiss of death for teen sales. Nike, on the other hand, was cool because it was identified with a white or black person, 12–21, athletic, urban and hip. New brands like Tommy Hilfiger and FUBU had usurped Levi Strauss's market position. Tommy was chosen as the favourite brand of teens in a 1999 American Express survey. Levis Strauss is attempting to fight back. They are getting in touch with the younger audience by setting up teen panels and keeping better tabs on the trend market. They have hired a new advertising agency and developed a Web presence, but only time will tell. A wakeup call to all businesses who need to stay fresh.

Brands Are Important to Kids

Kids want brands to:
- understand how they feel
- grow up with them
- know how to fit in
- understand that boys and girls are different
- be someone they can trust
- be fun

Source: Kidscope Kid Leo survey (a division of Leo Burnett); a survey of 700 school-aged kids world-wide in 1999, reprinted in *Strategy* magazine.

The days of the boomers setting pop culture trends is over, says Gerald Celente, editor of the *Trends* journal, quoted in a *Newsweek* article in January 2000, "Boomers are over the hill."

And this is now a problem for many successful brands who catered to the tastes of the boomers. Toyota is one of those brands. According to the same *Newsweek* article, Toyota has been very successful with boomers, who made the Camry America's top-selling car for the last three years. But now the average age of a Camry driver is 50 and a whole new generation of car buyers could think Toyota is for older people. To combat this Toyota has launched a youth marketing squad, the Genesis Initiative, to get in touch with the boomers' kids. The Genesis team is in a separate building, has decorated its offices like a teenager's bedroom and has built a new Web site, www.isthistoyota.com. It's working on product innovation to help attract younger buyers. While the team focuses on Generation X today they hope that Generation Y will see the brand in a different light as well. Success will be determined years from now given the time it takes to build new cars, but Toyota is even considering launching a new division to appeal to the younger car buyer as a shortcut to the problem. As one competitor said, until they have cars younger people like, advertising and Web sites are not going to make a difference. 1999's sales will be a test of that with the launch of the Echo, a new car designed to appeal to the oldest Generation Yers who are buying their first cars.

Car companies need to be aware of what these kids want in a car, given that over the next decade millions of new drivers will be entering the market. And their tastes are different from their parents. These young adults have been influenced by technology and want their cars to have a cooler look. But what is that look exactly? One young woman rejected the RAV 4 because she thought it was trying too hard to look cool and chose the Honda CRV instead. Generation Y has been influenced by different music and fashion styles and their ergonomic instincts have been honed by hours at the computer keyboard and with video game controls. These kids will be looking for styles that speak to them, not their parents. One family with two teenagers who were looking at cars were told by their kids that the Camry wasn't sporty enough. The kids preferred a Honda for its sporty looks and the image they wanted in a car. When it comes time for those two teens to buy cars,

Be youthful

Always have someone young in the room when you are planning new business ideas. You will hear a different perspective and get fresh ideas. They don't have years of adult rationale and baggage to block out new ideas. And younger people think and do things faster—they want to get on with it—which is a refreshing change in the business world.

Keep in touch with youth by creating a future panel. Gather a range of young people and put them in a room for a discussion, ask them to write you a letter to find out what they think about things.

Stop being an adult for a day. Walk in a kid's shoes to try to see things through young eyes. Open yourself up to a different point of view—watch YTV, go to a music store

(Continued on next page)

what brand do you think will be on their consideration list? And which one won't?

Kids can strike fear in the strongest brands. Brands and companies need to stay eternally young, otherwise they die off with their older customers. And most CEOs would agree that is a business model that doesn't work! Keeping young could mean cultivating lifelong preferences for a brand, as demonstrated by GM, or it could mean developing multiple strategies for the existing business.

Think of the Gap. The Gap has different stores, or what the retail world calls banners, for different styles, ages and price levels. The Gap runs the Gap stores, which offer stylish clothing basics, as well as Banana Republic (BR to aficionados), an urban style-conscious line of upscale professional merchandise, and Old Navy, a more youthful discount-clothing-basics store. Some retail analysts consider their good/better/best pricing and product strategy a key to their corporate success but you could also look at their business strategy as a generational strategy.

The young kids love Old Navy, teens love both Gap and Old Navy, and young professionals look to Banana Republic to fill a new place in their dressier work lives. From being a Baby Gap baby to wearing Gap khakis as a grandmother, the Gap has a cradle-to-grave strategy that gives them a bigger piece of the retail world than just being "teen experts." They manage their portfolio of brands to maximize a greater share of wallet from their customer families.

The old marketing adage "It's cheaper to keep an existing customer than to create a new one" is still true, and developing your future market through kids may be a viable way to look at your business. Maybe there is a sub brand or extension that would bring kids into the franchise today. Roots Kids is an example of building the Roots customer of the future as well as capitalizing on the demographic trend today. The same is true of Pottery Barn Kids. Both brands appeal to the boomer parents and the echo kids and this is good for business today and tomorrow.

Kidfluence is more than selling toys or nagging for a Disney vacation, it is about future customers and a company's ability to meet their needs and gain their business as purchasing adults.

The future market is theoretical and mind-boggling. And while planning for the future may seem akin to crystal-ball-gazing, every business should know where youth impacts its business. Given the strength of the new population boom, a business without a youth plan today may not be very successful in the future.

David Foot once said "Give your youth jobs or they will tear up the country or move away." We would add to that: Give your brands youth or they may shrivel up and die.

Be youthful
(Continued from previous page)

and talk to the staff, ask for music recommendations, eat at a fast food hangout and observe the kids, hear what they talk about and how they talk, go to a teen movieplex, check out a rave. Hang out in a playground or park and watch the activities.

Read a teen magazine. See the issues they care about, the things they worry about. Go to a Web site and chat room. Discover the way kids are interacting together. Read Harry Potter and watch *Buffy the Vampire Slayer*, listen to the BackStreet Boys.

SPEED READ SUMMARY

Kids represent the future, adult customers. The brands they hold dear when they are young could be the brands they prefer as adults.

- It's not just what kids buy today, it's the adults they become tomorrow that is important in business.
- Brand imprinting begins at a young age. The tween years seem particularly fertile for building brand equity, given the intellectual and social changes tweens experience.

- Keeping brands young is critical for the long-term health of the brands. Businesses need to plan ahead and nurture the brands and customers of the future
- In a world where brands rule, cradle-to-grave marketing maximizes a brand's returns.

11

The Adults
of Tomorrow

*I like the dreams of the future better
than the history of the past.*
— *Thomas Jefferson*

Fast forward to 2015. The bulge of Generation Y will then be 25. They will be in the workworld, making a living and building their adult lives. They may be getting married or living with a partner. They may be considering buying their first car and taking real vacations. They may be thinking of starting families or starting another degree. What kind of jobs will they have? What will they do in their spare time? Where will they be living? What dreams will they have? What will their lives hold? Will who they are today affect what they become tomorrow? And where and how will business be affected by these new adults?

One answer to all of these questions could be that this generation will act just like adults today—like their parents or Gen X. There is that old saying that the more things change the more they stay the same. And while that can be true of many lifestage experiences—such as starting a family—it may be that other experiences, such as buying a first car, furnishing a house or planning for a career, will be completely different, given the radical changes taking place today.

The influences of information and multimedia technology and the trend of growing older younger may create bigger differences in this group's experiences from those experienced by previous generations. And we have to remember it will be a different world that these new adults will be living in. The next two decades are expected to be a period of remarkable global transformation, say Peter Schwartz, Peter Leyden and Joes Hyatt, authors of *The Long Boom: A Vision for the Coming Age of Prosperity*. "No other age possessed the tools or the knowledge to do what we can do today." As Douglas Rushkoff, author of *Playing the Future: What We Can Learn from Digital Kids*, puts it: "The intensity of evolutionary change shows no sign of slowing down and people today need to adapt to the fact that we are changing so rapidly."

Generation Y is up for the challenge: Seventy-four per cent of teens believe they'll have a happy adulthood. Eighty-five per cent agree that "it is up to me to get what I want out of life." Generation Y plans on getting an education, building their own businesses and being happy— a pretty good scenario. Kids today, though more sophisticated, experienced and marketing-savvy, are still kids. They lead mostly happy lives and plan for happy futures. This youthful optimism is nothing new. When you are young you look forward to the changes and experiences of becoming an adult. We talked about kids wanting to be older as a sign of KAGOY, but when you get to be a teen growing up also means getting on to the good stuff: living on your own, making independent choices, hanging out with your friends whenever you want and falling in love. When you are young the world is your oyster. Of course, the sheer numbers of this group—eight million strong in Canada, comprising 26 per cent of the population—means that the Generation Y-ers will face stiff competition. Life's opportunities are influenced by how many people are born at the same time. Early boomers had a different work and economic experience than boomers born at the end of the cycle in the early 1960s. Many families in the 1970s and 1980s saw the dramatic difference of birth order when the eldest boomer prospered in the '70s, working and buying real estate, say, while the youngest was stalled entering the saturated workforce in the early '80s, or prevented from buying a home in the peak of the market in the late '80s. Those of Generation Y born 1980–1990 will benefit simply by being at the beginning of the bulge.

Whether there is competition or not, Generation Y will grow up in a period that is expected to bring economic prosperity, and a middle-class lifestyle, to people around the world. Three major trends will fuel this middle-class expansion: the computer and telecommunications technology, biotechnology, and new energy technologies, according to the authors of *The Long Boom*. They predict that the "Long Boom" (a 40-year period from 1980–2020) will result in a better world in which the new global economy will grow at unprecedented high rates, greatly expanding prosperity.

So it will be a good life for Generation Y. And a long one. The biotechnology dream is that the normal age span will increase to 120. This remarkable leap alone—from a life expectancy of 47 in 1900, to 75 in 2000, to 120 in 2020—will make life different for Generation Y. They will have a different view of time and of family relations. They will look forward to bouncing their great-great-grandchildren on their knees. But back to the mid-future. Today Generation Y speaks up, knows what they want, buys it if they want it. The world hears them and responds to them—will this change when they become adults? Given their clout, it's unlikely—so let's assume they will be demanding and vocal, experienced and knowledgeable, and not willing to wait for things.

Kids are optimistic about the future.

"Today's generation, and I don't care what country you're talking about, they want more than the passive experience, they want to control what goes on," said Peter Moore, the president of Sega of America, quoted in the *Toronto Star* in June 2000 on the subject of kids and media interactivity. "We're in a cultural swing where everything has to interact, everything has to connect." Think how this will impact the world. Take any issue, service or business, and imagine it 10, 15, 20 years from now. What will the youth of today think of it, given their cohort experience? In 2015, will a 25-year-old buy a car off a lot and shake hands with a salesperson after negotiating the right package? Will he kick the tires after making the decision on-line and in a virtual driving test? Will she stand in line at the local school to vote for a local politician when she has been e-mailing her votes and giving opinions to adults for years? Will the blue box program finally be fully adopted by the first generation of recyclers? Will a

20-year-old engage in face-to-face social activities or spend most of the time on-line in virtual situations?

Living On-Line

The cyber view of the world is likely scariest for people over a "certain" age. The amount of time people spend on the Internet is growing every day and it is believed that by 2015 everything will be doable on-line: business, shopping, communicating, playing. Think of the changes that will come with the advantages of increased speed and video images due to increased bandwidth. Virtual reality will become just a part of life in cyberspace, and Generation Y will take it in stride while the boomers will be widening the generation gap with "remember when" stories like "remember when we had to travel to a business meeting" or comments like "it used to take 3 months to do that kind of research properly." Access will change the way we live, the entertainment choices we make and the friendships we create. No matter what one's special interest is, the Internet will connect you with people who share it. If you like ballroom dancing you will easily be able to find the other ballroom dancers around the world with the help of a search engine.

The world will become smaller and more accessible with these connections and Generation Y will benefit from it all. In 2000, kids are already using the Internet to find jobs and create businesses. They are growing up participating in the world of e-commerce while boomers are still debating the security of using their credit cards on-line. Today kids and teens can be e-millionaires. A Toronto teen in grade eleven sold his Web site for over $1 million in 1999 and Researcher Computer Economics, Inc., a California-based research company, estimates that 8 per cent of all teens in the United States are making at least some money on the Net. This is the first generation to grow up in front of a computer screen, but it is also the first generation where wealth can be accumulated at such young ages. "Teens are becoming world entrepreneurs," says Nicholas Negroponte, founding director of MIT Media Lab.

But will, as some people fear, the children of 2015 and beyond be living a "virtual" life, stunted in their ability to make off-line connections? Most technology theorists believe, in contrast, that the amount of time you spend interfacing with a computer just makes you value real encounters all the more. "We will continue to watch live sports because it is one of the last areas of our life in which we can experience the unexpected, the improvisational," writes Mark Leyner in *Time* magazine. Julie Taymour, the director of the musical *The Lion King*, describes the live experience as a sensory experience which is not satisfied on-line. "What is the desire that entertainment fulfills? We want to be touched emotionally, be viscerally moved, perhaps have our minds challenged or at best blown. We travel to a different place when we enter the world of the storyteller. Some call it escape. Some call it experience." So while the cyber world plays an important role in the present and future of Generation Y, it does not limit their opportunities of experience, only adds to it. Our future prediction has Generation Y leaving their screens behind to enjoy a night out at the game or a show just as adults do today. The key difference for this generation is that a night out will be just one of the many leisure choices they have. Video on demand, customized TV, music compilations of their choice, are all new entertainment options available to Generation Y. The combination of expanded bandwidth and flat-screen technology will make home viewing a whole new theatre experience. Planning Generation Y adventures will be easy. It is the choosing that will be hard.

Closer to reality today, consider the changes in the retail industry alone and the impact these changes will have on consumers of the future. The big shift from the downtown shopping district to the suburban mall in the 1970s, to the introduction of big box and specialty store formats of the 1980s, will be overshadowed by the current shift we are experiencing from bricks and mortar to clicks and virtual storefronts. Shopping behaviour did not fundamentally change when someone drove to the mall instead of driving downtown—only the location and size of the building did. The shopping experience of being inside versus outside changed but people still drove, parked, walked around and were entertained by the social experience of it all. But retailing today and in the future will include both buildings and cyberspace—two different types of shopping behaviour. How you buy and what you buy on-line is different from a live shopping trip. Looking at pictures of shoes is different than trying them on and walking around in them. Picking up a cantaloupe, smelling it and pushing your thumb in the end is a freshness test that cannot be duplicated through the computer. And while the shopping experiences on-line are going to get better and multisensory, being in a physical store will always be a different experience than being in a virtual shop. A retail business of the future will need to understand and manage both customer behaviours to be successful. Understanding the differences in customer motivation and behaviour in both scenarios will be a competitive advantage that will distinguish more companies in the future.

Many assumptions have been made from generation to generation on what consuming behaviour will be like. For years department stores have just assumed that people will always need to shop there. The basic design and offering of the department store is virtually unchanged since its invention. One wonders if that will still be true in 2015 with Generation Y, who grew up buying on-line and having things delivered to their door. Will the first generation to have specialty retailers designing for their needs alone accept the experience of a department store with broad assortments, little service, and many time-consuming checkouts? Will walking from department to department seem reasonable when they operate on warp speed and multitask as easily as breathing? Boomers are comfortable in department stores because they were the convenience stores of their youth and adulthood. Buying so many things in one place was considered convenient. In 1985 it was convenient, in 2000 it was convenient. But you have to wonder if it will still be convenient in 2015. To the boomers and Generation X maybe. To Generation Y? Who knows.

Future Work: What Will It be to Generation Y?

Being an adult means Work. What will work be to Generation Y?

The number-one trend of the late 1990s was self-reliance, according to the 1996 *Roper Youth Report*, which tracks attitudinal changes over time in North America. As North American boomers grew disenchanted with institutions and their failure to support them, and were disenfranchised by large companies who downsized their way through the 1980s and '90s, they grew increasingly self-sufficient. The boomers' children will have grown up in an environment that taught them to take care of themselves. Whether that self-reliance is due to the effects of job instability or to the self-confidence kids gained by mastering technology and harnessing information, this generation is *planning* on taking care of themselves. When choosing a life work, this self-reliance will likely be a key factor. In 1998 about 18 per cent of Canadians were entrepreneurs.

According to Statistics Canada, this has increased from 12 per cent in 1976. In the *YTV Kid &Tween Report*, 43 per cent of tweens claimed they wanted to start their own business. And 31 per cent of the youth polled in *Realm* magazine in 1998 said that given a choice their first pick of a profession would be entrepreneur.

Futurist Richard Worzel believes the trend of self-reliance will continue with this generation as they will work in an age of entrepreneurialism. "This generation will need to be self-sufficient and have a variety of skills," states a booklet on preparing kids for the future that Worzel created with Trimark Investment Management Inc. "The future will offer more opportunity and less security no matter what career your children pursue. Long gone will be the days of working for one company. Like free agents our kids will have to continually entice their employers to pick up their option for the following year. In our future, our children will need to sell their abilities on a regular basis." Don Tapscott called this approach to work "molecularization" in his book *Growing Up Digital*. "Rather than working like a cog in the wheel, the N-Gen worker will be comfortable working more like a molecule—a business unit of one." Worzel explains that the Generation Yers' ability in information-handling and their independence and autonomy will allow them to easily work in non-traditional fluid structures.

To illustrate his point Worzel developed a scenario of the future.

Here is an excerpt from Trimark Investment on how he sees the future workworld:

The Future of Work—Getting Kids Ready

Thirty-two-year-old Mike Brown hangs up the phone. He's a self-employed marketing consultant who has just landed an invitation to bid on a job he knows very little about. The assignment has come from Karen, a contract marketer for a real estate development group. Mike's spent a year promoting his services to Karen in a low-key way, and it's finally resulted in a potentially significant invitation to bid on a project for a new supported living community—a field Mike knows nothing about. To assemble the proposal, he'll need to call on his informal network of self-employed associates. The research that needs to be done will be quarterbacked by Mike, but he'll hand off the writing, graphic design, production and Web site development to other members of his network. They all work in close co-operation by video-phone, even though they live in different time zones on widely separated continents.

He thinks for a moment, then says to Alfred, his computer 'butler' and invaluable assistant, "Initiate database search on assisted-living communities for mixed groups composed on individuals over 65, and families of children with disabilities. Search Statistics Canada, U.S. Library of Congress, UNESCO. End list. Seek additional databases. Ask for information from the Rehabilitation Centre for Children, the Canadian Association of Retired Persons. End list. Seek other sources. Limit total fees paid to $100. Begin search."

Satisfied that his computer has received the request, Mike then calls one of his regular subcontractors on the phone: "Nina, can you contact the team we used on our NASA tourism project and tell them I need them to do some work on spec for a proposal?" He has Alfred download the details to Nina's computer butler. After some small talk Nina signs off and gets busy.

Next, Mike spends an hour surfing the Net, looking for ideas. It's something he can't delegete because he's not sure what he's looking for until he sees it.

Mike's working world is an unstructured one based on research, a steep learning curve, a network of friends and connections, and a reputation carefully nurtured over time. He responds with great speed to new challenges, and is constantly, opportunistically looking for ways to spread his network of both suppliers and clients.

Mike took his BA in English literature to his first job with a software company when he left university in 2012. It was a great place to start because the people were all upbeat and smart. They preferred to teach the specifics of marketing their products to someone creative and with a broad range of skills, rather than hire someone who had studied marketing but had a narrow range of experiences and was unable to think independently.

While Mike enjoyed this environment, after a while it started to chafe. He often wanted to do things his way but had to defer to his employers, and when the firm made a big hit, he didn't share in the rewards. Meanwhile, one of his more entrepreneurial friends had become a multimillionaire by starting his own company and then taking it public, so Mike eventually left and started his own organization.

Mike's still a one-person show, even though his annual gross billings are now in the millions of dollars. He has no employees—only a machine called Alfred, his computer assistant. What he does have is a network of people who are very talented, trust his judgement, and are happy to subcontract for him, as he's happy to subcontract for them.

When he was studying Jane Eyre *in university, Mike never expected to wind up running a marketing company, but he loves it.*

Source: The Future of Work—Getting Kids Ready—Trimark Legacy for Learning. *Trimark Investment Management Inc.*

Stats Canada claims that 60 per cent of all employment growth between 1990–98 came from self-employment, and Worzel expects self-employment to make up more than one-third of jobs in Canada by 2020. Tapscott summarizes, "N-Geners will prefer to create new businesses than change old, big ones. By growing their own businesses they can control their destiny—a N-Gen requirement." But even with a major trend towards entrepreneurial ventures, some big business will continue to prosper, though it will change. Some think that just as the Internet created an infomocracy, big business will be democratized as well with the elimination of the middleman. "Everybody wants everything faster with less hassle. The factory walls will be broken down." Possibly just another example of Generation Y controlling their destiny.

Blending Work and Life

Work affects life. The change in the work world will create many different life situations. The trend of more people working in alternate

New Work Environment

A study of college graduates in 1999 in the United States listed what priorities the recent grads had in choosing their first jobs. Topping the list was a fun work environment, followed by growth opportunities, a competitive salary and diversity in projects. A fun work environment meant they wouldn't be stuck in cubicles but would be able to communicate and interact with their

(Continued on next page)

**New Work
Environment**
(Continued from previous page)

peers and contribute
ideas. This access is
what Generation Y
has been brought up
on and will naturally
expect, and demand
from any working
environment.

work situations, whether from home businesses or telecommuting, and the new-found flexibility in work is expected to continue. This lifestyle or workstyle influences house design, furniture styles, clothing requirements and daily transportation needs. Work of the future can happen anywhere.

One futurist in a special edition of *Time* magazine blue-skyed about beaming in phone conferences so colleagues are projected full-size on a living-room wall. Or having text appear like a teleprompter in front of the golf cart making note referral easy while talking with clients halfway around the world. No need to go into the office when you can network like that without a commute. Generation Y will experience most of these things and it will seem natural, not Jetson-like. One of the future experts states that between one-third and one-half of North Americans will live outside metropolitan and suburban areas by 2010 a reversal of current population trends. John Naisbitt in *Megatrends 2000* describes this as the electronic heartland—a trend where people can choose to live where they want due to links in technology and telecommunications.

A change in work also impacts personal finances. If we move to a world of networked free agents and independent businesses working on projects together, the short-term work contracts will reduce the ability to plan and predict long-term cash flow. The financial industry will have to consider how this will impact buying, renting and leasing options.

The new economy has seen more people get rich younger, as age and experience are not the requirements for financial success. Competency and ideas will reign in the new workplace. Generation Y share the belief that knowledge knows no boundaries and the new business elite will be those who started a successful business and made a lot of money from selling it.

Companies may not be built to last but built to flip. This approach to entrepreneurship would appeal to Generation Y given their need for speed and their change-adapted ways.

Global Inclusiveness

A world of free agents working in networked teams could also change the way people relate to each other. This work dynamic requires a combination of flexibility, independence and teamwork. These developed skills could influence how adults interact with the world at large, possibly creating a more tolerant, inclusive atmosphere. Mike Farrell, the creative insight provocateur at The NRG Group says, "Generation Y has been brought up as an accepted part of society and they will likely be generally more liberal and accepting of others because of that." Defining Generation Y is "connexity," according to a Saatchi and Saatchi Advertising agency study. Connexity is the importance of staying connected in order to grow. Kids' digital experiences today allow them to connect with different people on an equal footing, creating a sense of inclusion rather than exclusion.

Bev Topping, the founder of *Today's Parent* magazine, sees a global vision being developed with kids today. "Communicating with people we can't see will become the norm (in this global vision). Maybe this will help our children's world be less prejudicial, since they will establish relationships with others before they see a face. In that way, technology may make the world a better place—finally teaching us that race and religion needn't get in the way of helping us really connect with others and build better communities in which to live."

All generations can see the rational and physical improvements that technology has created but it seems that Generation Y will benefit most from growing up not knowing how to live any other way. The benefits of reduced prejudice, global inclusiveness and a need to connect may be the key difference Generation Y can make in future world harmony.

Assuming our society continues prospering, the current youth generation could experience a need to consume that surpasses their parents.

More Still

If prosperity continues, the "more" generation could have a need to consume that exceeds their boomer parents. Their addiction to change and speed could fuel an acceleration of consumption. They have adapted to change so well that it is just natural to want more. They grew up in an environment that expected the world to progress.

But how far can the acceleration go? When is improved really, and finally, improved? Can "more" and "better" ever end?

One wonders when it comes to the improvement and advancement of technology how our world will operate. One future vision has computer functions fitting on a chip the size of a screw. However, Stephen Bayley, a British futurist, believes the rate of change is slowing down. "Look at Sony. Between 1955 and 1985 Sony introduced a new product type every year. They haven't been able to maintain that momentum." "There is enough clutter already," Bayley continues. "So much of our civilization is based on restless neophilia. I tend to think the big quest in the future is going to be for quality of experience, not novelty of merchandise."

There are others, like Bayley, who believe that the acceleration of "more" cannot possibly continue. Ad Busters is one group that believes there is a backlash trend happening with the younger generations. In the book *Culture Jam: The Uncooling of America*, Kalle Lasn, a Canadian activist and founder of *Adbusters* magazine, which satirizes commercials, claims our culture is rich but also sick, miserable and bloated from excess. "Our emotions, personalities, and core values are under siege from media and cultural forces. A continuous product message has woven itself into the very fabric of our existence." Writer Naomi Klein also made this the subject of her book *No Logo*. "A backlash is coming," she believes, "because there is a growing resistance among youth to the corporate homogenization of global culture." Carol Holst, founder of the Seeds of Simplicity, a simplicity help group in Los Angeles, agrees with both sentiments and estimates that between 15 and 20 per cent of people entering their twenties are rejecting possession obsession.

But others think the backlash is not against brands and consumption but about control. In conversation with The NRG Group, they felt that "when it comes to kids rebelling and protesting, they are rebelling against the idea of who's in charge of these global entities and how they are becoming irrelevant." With kids and especially teens it's all about being relevant to them and having a dialogue with them. The backlash comes when this vocal, empowered generation feels out of step and wants to bring the higher powers back to grassroots action.

Improvement in the world is not necessarily materialistic. The natural expectation from human beings is that things continue to get better. It is the basis of evolution. But how much better can our lives get? What will a new quality of life be? No one really knows for sure.

But for Generation Y the next few decades will continue to offer them "more" through better lives, due to the changes beyond computer technology and into nanotechnology and biotechnology. Both technologies will dramatically change our physical worlds. Nanotechnology will change the way we view manufacturing, as things will be built atom by atom. All of today's conventional thinking about size, speed, efficiency, waste will be affected by this new industry. Biotechnology will be enhancing our lives with new medicine and non-invasive treatments, and stretching our life expectancy. The desire and need for "more" will translate into longer, healthier and more youthful lives for Generation Y.

The Instant World

Generation Y does not wait. They grew up with the technological control to make things happen and they grew up knowing instant macaroni and cheese takes only three minutes instead of the torturous wait for the seven-minute variety.

The food industry will be different in 2015. Generation Y is growing up in houses where few people cook. Food businesses are fuelling this trend with easy-to-prepare foods and take-home meals.

Cooking is considered to be in risk of possible extinction. Since moms went to work in full force, kids started to see less scratch cooking in their homes. There is still a segment of kids learning to cook, but most are not, says Daphna Rabinovitch, associate food editor at *Canadian Living* magazine. Evidence comes in the size of today's cookbooks—they are noticeably longer than they were even 20 years ago. "That's because the writers can't assume the reader will understand cooking terms such as scald, fold, etc. These directions used to be summed up in one word— now they take two sentences." Cooking is the perfect metaphor for how life has changed in the last 50 years. Consider the lowly casserole. There was a time when homemade macaroni and cheese was considered a convenience food of sorts. Sure, it took time for Mom to make the cheese sauce and boil the pasta, but the beauty of it was she could double, even triple, the recipe and freeze if for instant dinners during the week. That worked until the late 1960s when Kraft's macaroni and cheese dinner hit the supermarket shelves. Conveniently packaged, priced right and easy to prepare (15 minutes from start to finish) it became a staple in homes and dorms across the country. Now, even Kraft Dinner has evolved to meet the demand of today's hurried pace. No longer wanting to stand over the stove for seven minutes, we've got a three-minute, single-serving version, Easy Mac. Before you can get the ketchup out of the fridge, dinner's ready.

In the late 1980s food companies started to witness a trend they dubbed "speed scratch" which involves taking some prepared ingredients and adding to them to make the new version of home cooking. In the future our definition of homemade will be radically different from what was "home cookery" which most boomers grew up with in the fifties. A look at the chart entitled "Homemade Then and Now" tells the story. Other convenience foods, such as home-meal replacements, are also growing in popularity. "Today's parents still cling to the idea of eating together. Canadians think that's very important," says Rabinovitch. But with more dual-income families, there is less time to

Homemade Then and Now
Its definition changes with time

In 1950	In 2000
SPAGHETTI SAUCE	
crushed own tomatoes and added own spices and vegetables	buy bottled sauce, add pre-packaged veggies, microwave
LEMON PIE	
squeezed lemons by hand made pie crust from scratch	buy powdered crystal filling and frozen pie crust, bake
COFFEE CAKE	
made dough from yeast, added basic ingredients	buy refrigerated dough, put in oven
TURKEY STUFFING	
ground bread/crackers by hand, cooked and added basic ingredients	buy ready-made stuffing, cook it on stove top

prepare meals. Home-meal replacements solve that problem. "Mövenpick and President's Choice have had a big impact with their home-meal replacements (family-sized lasagna, Shepherd's Pie)." It's a trend that will continue to grow as caterers and food manufacturers join forces to create other pre-packaged ensembles.

It is possible, then, that when the Generation Y sits down to eat as adults or as part of a family the food will not have been cooked in the home. The *Time* magazine "Visions of the 21st Century" special section talked about the kitchen of the future being a small room where food is opened, warmed and readied for the table. The standard icon of Mom in the kitchen that most boomers grew up with won't represent the moms of the year 2015.

Generation Y Families

Families are very important to Generation Y. They speak of family activities as an important part of their life and most see their parents as their role models and heroes. Even so, will this generation be able to maintain relationships when they expect everything to happen instantly? As discussed earlier, half of this generation grew up in divorced families and 22 per cent in single-parent households, so the ability to form lasting relationships may be underdeveloped or extremely valued. As we know, in 2000 the trend is for young adults to delay marriage and starting families. Women used to get married at the age of 21; over the last two decades the average age for a bride has increased, to 25 and then to 27. It is not uncommon for couples today to start their families after the age of 30 or 35. It is interesting to think that in the era of kids getting older younger they don't necessarily move into life stages faster. They extend their adolescence as long as they can. One writer said that coming of age is becoming a lifelong process. Kay Hymowitz, an author who writes about the KAGOY phenomenom in her book titled *Ready or Not*, calls this trend postadolescence. She claims that post-adolescence emerged with Generation X and describes the Gen X-ers as tired of their sophistication and disillusioned. "They can permit themselves friendships but not love affairs, cohabitation but not marriage, sociability but not interdependence."

Gen X and Y share the same childhood experience where one of two marriages break up, 60 per cent remarry and 50 per cent break up again. Understandably, these generations may believe that relationships are not forever, or at least very complicated to maintain. The combined families that are the result of multiple marriages may expand the definition of family. A family in the 2000s includes steps, halfs, halfs again, four or more grandparents, dozens of aunts, uncles and cousins. On one hand nuclear families are shrinking, but on the other, family connections are expanding.

Generation Y may need to simplify by growing up with access to multimedia, technology and reams of information, Generation Y are good editors who can scan a situation and determine what is relevant. "We are coming to understand that what we so valued as an attention span is something entirely different from what we thought. The skill to be valued in the twenty-first century is not the length of the attention span but the ability to multitask—to do many things at once well." Douglas Rushkoff, whose theories and ideas in the book *Playing the Future* are fascinating and mind-boggling, believes that "the ability to process visual information quickly will enable the worker of the future to cope with the information overload." He uses the example of how we intuitively understand comic strip symbols to explain how icons play an important role in meaning and understanding. Whether it be two people with two bubbles in one frame that we understand as dialogue or curved lines behind characters indicating action, we process the information with the correct meaning. This instant comprehension will be welcomed in a world drowning in information. Icons allow us to skim yet retain understanding.

In the world of 2015 brands will be important because brands are an "instant read." They are shorthand for personality, point of view and status. Instead of a world of no logos as envisioned by Naomi Klein, logos may hold even more value. In an instant world, brand icons will be a much needed editing tool, for people overloaded with information. An easily recognized icon instantly represents the meaningfulness and desirability of the brand. Brands will be a speed read for those in a hurry.

But who knows for sure? After all, with a little imagination anyone can paint a picture of the future. It just takes imagination. It can be entertaining. It involves playing a game of "what ifs." It can be light-hearted conversation for any group of friends or family to have. But if you are in business today it is prudent to be creating a future scenario for Generation Y in 2015. The Achilles' heel of most businesses is that they are run by people aged 30 plus. The more we age the less we connect with youth. Losing this connection can be painful or even fatal for business.

SPEED READ SUMMARY

- Kids of the future will live in a dramatically different world than the one boomers grew up in. Life spans will increase, technology will continue to make things possible that we cannot imagine today and kids will work and play in an on-line world that we are only beginning to appreciate.
- Kids today are an example of the natural progress of evolution. Douglas Rushkoff says, "The intensity of evolutionary change shows no sign of slowing down and people today need to adapt to the fact that we are changing so rapidly."

- The "more" generation will continue with more work choices, more entertainment and lifestyle options and more prosperity.
- The hope is that Gen Y will also be more tolerant and inclusive, given their global awareness and connections.
- Those who can adapt to speed and the scanning and editting of information will succeed. Brands will be important "speed reads" in the future as people drown in the overavailability of information.

12

Coming Full Circle

Kids are advance scouts.
They already are—what we must become.
—Douglas Rushkoff

What a thought-provoking statement. If it is true, we have come full circle from a century ago. Adults and children are once again separated by purpose, playing different roles in their changing world. The millennial twist is that kids are leading the charge.

As we face the future, we see that today's kids are better equipped than adults to deal with the momentous change that is facing our society. We have only begun to absorb the opportunity of the computer age. The impact of the personal computer is said to be of the same if not greater magnitude as the printing press. Since we didn't live through that change, it is hard to imagine what that invention meant to people at that time. They were likely excited, but a bit apprehensive, about the possibilities opening up before them. They probably worried that life was moving too fast, that things were changing too much or that the technology would control them. Legitimate concerns—past and present. The wisdom of hindsight shows us they had little to worry about.

Move ahead 20 years from today and imagine looking back on the turn of the millennium. What will people be saying about the adults and kids who lived through it? Will they wonder how half the population lived with only one computer in the house? Will they debate the benefits of our simpler life? And what will they see as defining social issues of our times? Mass marketing or permissive parenting? Internet access or lack thereof?

It is hard to imagine that access of any kind will be seen as a problem when it is the one thing most adults crave. They like the control and independence access guarantees—it is something we all grow up wanting. Kids today, who have had access most of their lives, are not likely to deny it to their children. It will be accepted as the norm—whether it is access to the Internet or access to family decision-making. As for time spent with computers, it won't even be an issue. By that time the computer chip will be ubiquitous, an inescapable part of our daily routine, one our kids will be eminently comfortable living and teaching adults about. According to Don Tapscott, author of *Growing Up Digital*, "Children are an authority about the biggest revolution in society."

Vicky Saunders, a founder of The NRG Group puts it another way. In her opinion adults are immigrating into this world while the kids are native to it.

Tomorrow's World

The acceleration of "more" reflects the speed at which our world is changing and is just preparation for the times ahead. It is neither a good thing nor a bad thing. It is evolution.

We have evolved to the state we need to be. Imagine the family from the 1800s who didn't travel more than 30 miles in a lifetime. They could not deal with the world today. Our experiences and lifestyle changes over the last few decades have helped us acclimatize to face tomorrow's world. As families, we have been moving toward this goal, first encouraging our kids to participate in decision-making and now looking to our kids to show us the way. This is new territory for adults. Those who don't adapt, who continue to operate at the pace they grew up with, will be left behind and the generation gap will widen. Technology could very well be the driving force that tears the ages and generations apart. As parents, educators, policy makers and business people, we need to be preparing kids for their future success. This future demands one be skilled in multimedia applications, multi-tasking and information-processing.

Is this a good thing? We always philosophically come back to this question. We acknowledge that things are the way they are today, but does that mean we should accept it—and happily?

Look at it from this perspective: Would children benefit from adults interrupting the speed of change? Can we go back to a simpler time or rest on our laurels? Not likely. The changes we are facing in the "Long Boom" will be the most dramatic yet. The chips have left the station and the computer age is moving full steam ahead.

Consider this, too: most of what our kids will know we can't even imagine yet. We still have more potential than reality—a frightening thought for adults who are scared of the unknown. The kids aren't afraid though. They are looking forward to their lives and the opportunities before them. Why should parents let today's issues cloud their kids' futures when we know the world is going to be so different tomorrow?

Much of what our children will learn in the future, we would find unimaginable today.

Another fact to consider is that we need to evolve as part of our natural progression as a human race. Our brains do change over time and learn new ways. The more we learn through personal experience the more our brain *can* learn. The more we interact, the greater our ability for more complex interactions. This is the wonderful thing about humans. We continue to learn and grow. We should celebrate this truth, not lament it.

What's Enough?

Should more be stopped? Should parents limit the demands for more or is "the pursuit of more" as much a part of living today as the pursuit of liberalism was to the boomers? Should businesses not encourage consumption through promotions, packaging and advertising to kids? Maybe a call for moderation is good advice—as it is in most situations. Getting or having "stuff" is not critical to life skills. Having experiences is. Parents need to determine their own way through the balance of stuff versus life experiences to develop the kid becoming the adult of the future.

But beyond the scope of the parents, we still live in a consuming and corporate culture. Are kids just a target market or are they living the new lifestyle? By exposing their business potential in this book, are we endorsing the idea of marketing to children?

Parents must take an active role in deciding how they wish to handle the impact of marketing to kids.

We believe that kids are a consumer group with needs and wants—and they have been for many years and generations to the traditional toy and cereal industries. We are neither for nor against marketing to children, but we firmly believe that kids should not be viewed as business pawns or exploited for corporate greed. Kids are one opportunity that responsible businesses can assess within the scope of their total business. It is up to parents, not industries, to determine what is best for their families. Parents can control exposure and they can control spending; these are choices they make based on their experiences and beliefs. Businesses make decisions that are right for their businesses. With respect and common sense both sides will benefit.

Kids will want to have a say as well. Kids today want to be heard and they will make sure that corporations listen. Kids today are empowered and are experiencing the world bottom up, rather than top down. The Internet has changed the conversation between business and kids. Kids are knocking on the world's door, saying speak *with* me—not at me.

Kids have influence and money largely because their parents and business gave this to them. Kids buy things because we live in a consuming culture. Kids change, grow and learn new things because we as humans need to evolve. We move forward, rather than stand still. The world is unfolding as it should. So why does it feel so different to the adults?

Because the role of boomer adults is changing. Up till now it's always been about the boomers, and now it's starting to be all about their kids. And what makes this change even more difficult is that boomers identify themselves as being young and the next generation now rightfully owns it. Boomers are struggling to hold on to their youth—the way they dress, the music they listen to, the exercise and nutrition routines they follow, even the plastic surgery and laser eye treatments they demand. The authors of *Rocking the Ages—the Yankelovich Report on Generational Marketing* wrote, "Even in the throes of nostalgia, Boomers still think of themselves as young. When asked to describe themselves Boomers aligned more closely with younger Generation Xers than with the ways the older Mature Generation described themselves. Boomers want to be, in the words of an old Bob Dylan tune, 'Forever Young'."

The boomers are the first adults to want to identify with their kids rather than create a separate "adult" world. Boomers don't want to be left behind. Being involved in their kids' lives is one way they get to hang on to the feeling of being young and being "in the know" of the latest in pop culture and technology. They have been responsible for driving the consumer market for so long they do not want to be usurped by a new generation.

In the first part of this book, we described how the boomers' ideals created great movement in the last half of the century. Change happened with the boomers because they decided early on that the old rules no longer applied to them. We concluded that kidfluence began when the boomers' children began to live the change their parents eagerly embraced. Boomers wanted more and demanded it—Generation Y grew up getting more, thrived on it and today are driving it. Now we see the circle completing itself and a new shape emerging—*that the boomer parents will live the change their kids eagerly embrace.* 88 million kids. One generation full circle to a new generation. More kids. More money. More power. Generation Y—The "more" generation. Welcome to the reality of kidfluence.

Case Studies

CASE STUDY: DELIAS

Background
— Founded 1993
— Went Public 1996
— Founded by Steve Kahn and Chris Edgar
— Started from $100,000 in savings and $1 million startup from family and friends
— Corporate Offices in West Village, New York City
— 1500 employees

www.delias.com

Business Concept
- Saw girls as an untapped market. Thought girls were interested in fashion, liked looking at fashion magazines and going through their mothers' catalogues, so they developed something for that niche

  "Naysayers never dissuaded me.
  I was convinced this overlooked niche had potential."

  —*Steve Kahn*

- "Downtown style everywhere." Cutting-edge style with mail-order distribution focused on Gen Y girls (target 10–24, core focus 12–17)
- Sell clothes, accessories, home furnishings
- Founders' vision "We are going to win this generation"
- Tested the concept by promoting the catalogue through placing direct-response ads in the classified sections of *Seventeen, Mademoiselle, Cosmo*. Thousands of responses encouraged them to launch the catalogue

Success Factors
1. Grassroots introduction (no mass advertising in the beginning; now they use print and on-line ads)
   - Believe girls shared their discovery of Delias with friends
   - Arranged catalogue drops at schools
   - Web presence fuels discovery
2. Unique product—stuff teens can't find easily in their markets

3. The voice and personality: "We speak the language of our customer"
   - Is smart and in open dialogue with the customer
   - Company itself staffs young people and young reps from high school and college students take the orders over the phone. The order form is accessible and helpful (e.g., giving tips on how to order pants)
   - The catalogues show models who look like real girls rather than supermodels
4. Getting on-line with the first generation to grow up shopping on-line (four of their own sites):
   - Gurl.com
   - droog.com
   - contentsonline.com
   - store.yahoo.com/stores
5. Growing list of customer names and contacts (acquisitions added six million names)

Business Results
- 1996: $30 million sales
- 1999: $5.5 million profit on $150 million sales
- Projected to triple sales 1999-2000
- Delias database of 10 million names
- Total corporate database of 16 million names
- Stock price rose from $4 to $32 in 1999
- Retail expansion from clicks to mortar: Delias has 17 stores now and plans to have 30 by 2001
- In 1997 bought gurl.com, a popular fashion chat and game site Opened second channel with launch of its own Web site with news, entertainment, catalogue request, e-mail, on-line shopping in 1997
- Launched Droog, a catalogue for boys
- Bought a mall chain of young men's fashion stores called Screem

Case Study: YTV

Background

Launched in 1988 by Rogers, CUC and a group of independent producers.

- Owned by Corus Entertainment today (who also owns part or all of Teletoon, Family Channel, Treehouse TV, Nelvana Animation)

Why a kid channel?

- The launch group felt that kids were exposed to too much American programming
- Lack of programs available to kids at all hours of the day

Success Factors

At the start:

1. Revenue from advertisers poured back into original programming
2. Getting the Right Properties: *Goosebumps* and *Teenage Mutant Ninja Turtles*
3. Fine-Tuning the Target Focus
   - Original kid mandate, ages 2–17, resulted in a large and fragmented audience
   - Focus on tweens brought an identity and personality to the station

Continuing today:

4. Getting Close to the Viewer and Really Understanding Them
   - "Keep it weird" was the brand idea that connected with tweens and kids
   - An on-going panel helps us stay in touch with our audience
   - Always having great programs that connect with the kids, e.g.: Pokémon, Big Comfy Couch
5. Gathering Customer Data to Share with Advertisers
   "The *Kid & Tween Report* captures behaviour and attitudes which helps us build our relationship with kids and helps our advertisers understand the impact of their financial power."
6. Refining audience description to the core of kids aged 6–11.
7. Expanding into Other Media Channels to Extend Brand Reach
   - Launched magazine in spring 1999 in partnership with Paton Marketing, a division of *Today's Parent Group*. Published three times a year and distributed through Pizza Hut and Chapters and newstands
   - Travelling Road Shows like Wow and Psykoblast
   - Web site entertains and extends brand reach beyond TV hours

Business Results

- 96 per cent of English Canada household penetration or 8 million households
- Average weekly reach is 2 million kids
- Kids spend an average of 4 hours and 15 minutes a week with YTV (up from one hour in 1988)
- Surveys show that Canadians kids watch YTV more than any other channel and kids claim "YTV is their favourite channel"
- 6.5 million hits a week on the Web site where kids spend an average of 12 minutes, which is considered a record!

CASE STUDY:
PUTTING A KID PANEL TOGETHER

In-Sync, a consumer planning and research company in Toronto, designed the kid panel for YTV. Laura Baehr of YTV and Allison Gentile of In-Sync shared these tips.

Panel Process

- To get the kids, the research company issued a questionnaire which received around 300 replies.
- That group was culled to around 50 who came in for personal interviews.
- 12 panel members were picked to participate in four sessions over a year.
- Criteria for selection was "great, average kids." They needed to have confidence to speak up, and be lateral thinkers, and commit to participating for a year on the panel.

How to Run a Panel Session

- Start the kick-off meeting with a pizza-and-pop get-to-bond time, a warm-up for the real sessions that follow. "It was important to get the kids used to each other and us before we launched into the real work."
- The 90-minute sessions cover a wide range of topics. Sometimes assignments have been given ahead of time and the kids' work will be reviewed together. Other times the group will discuss the subject of the moment that will help YTV with programming or media and promotion ideas.
- A research team that understands kids and can keep them involved and productive for 90 minutes. "Kids' short attention spans require that you keep variety in the mix. You have to cram a lot into 10 minutes, before you lose their attention."
- The research team also has to have the expertise to pick the right kids because the panel is only as good as the quality of the participants.

Biggest Surprise

- The prestige of being on the panel.
- Kids think it is really cool that they are linked to the television network.
- "It was really amazing how many parents wanted their kids on the panel. Maybe they thought they were going to get on TV?"

CASE STUDY:
EVALUATING KIDS AS PART OF YOUR BUSINESS PLAN

If you are a business-person, how do you quantify the real economic impact of kids, tweens and teens?

There are many variables to consider in your analysis. Look beyond the broad classification of kids and think specifically about the following topics:

Age

Not surprisingly, older kids have more money. They have more in their pockets and they spend more. Younger kids impact the household grocery budget from a very young age because they are with their parents in the shopping cart. Branding may be more effective after the age of seven.

Gender

Boys buy more fast food, girls buy more cosmetics. Both girls and boys buy music and clothes but girls are over-retailed in fashion.

The Business Category

Kids spend on different things and in varying frequency. In some businesses they participate as secondary consumers and in others as influencers, but they always make a difference. Ask yourself:

- Do kids buy my product or service?
- Do kids use my product or service?
- Do kids benefit from my product or service?

Location

Kids have preferences on where they like to shop. They shop where they feel comfortable. And they influence where their parents go.

Kids Grow Up

Future customers? Kids are brand-aware and savvy at younger ages. Their impressions of your brand may start from the age of seven.

Ask Yourself:

1. Can I make my brand stronger by having a relationship with kids earlier?
2. Do I need to have a communication plan for kids?
3. Do I need to investigate this opportunity with research?

Bibliography

Books

Acuff, Dan S. *What Kids Buy and Why: The Psychology of Marketing to Kids*. New York: The Free Press, 1997.

Bennett, Holly, and Teresa Pitman. *Steps and Stages: From 9 to 12—The Preteen Years*. Toronto: Key Porter Books, 1998.

Bennett, Steve. *The Plugged-In Parent: What You Should Know About Kids and Computers*. New York: Random House, 1998.

Del Vecchio, Gene. *Creating Ever-Cool: A Marketer's Guide to a Kid's Heart*. Gretna, Ill: Pelican Publishing, 1997.

Douglas, Ann. *The Complete Idiot's Guide to Canada in the '60s, '70s, and '80s*. Scarborough: Prentice Hall Canada, 1999.

Dryden, Ken, and Roy MacGregor. *Home Game: Hockey and Life in Canada*. Toronto: McClelland & Stewart, Inc., 1991.

Edwards, Peggy, Miroslava Lhotsky, and Judy Turner. *The Healthy Boomer: A No-Nonsense Midlife Healthy Guide for Women and Men*. Toronto: McClelland & Stewart, Inc., 1999.

Foot, David K., and Daniel Stoffman. *Boom Bust and Echo 2000*. Toronto: Macfarlane Walter & Ross, 1998.

Harris, Judith Rich. *The Nurture Assumption: Why Children Turn Out the Way They Do*. New York: Touchstone, 1998.

Hersch, Patricia. *A Tribe Apart: A Journey into the Heart of American Adolescence*. New York: Fawcett Book Group, 1998.

Hymowitz, Kay S. *Ready or Not: Why Treating Children as Small Adults Endangers Their Future and Ours*. New York: The Free Press, 1999.

Jenkins, Henry. *The Children's Culture Reader*. New York: New York University Press, 1998.

Kawasaki, Guy. *Rules for Revolutionaries*. New York: Harper Business, 1999.

Lasn, Kalle. *Culture Jam:The Uncooling of America*. Eagle Brook, 1999.

McDonnell, Kathleen. *Kidculture: Children, Adults & Popular Culture*. Toronto: Second Story Press, 1994.

McNeal, James U. *Kids as Customers*. Lanham, MD: Lexington Books, 1992.

McNeal, James U. *The Kids Market: Myths and Realities.* Ithaca, NY: Paramount Market Publishing, 1999.

Naisbitt, John. *Megatrends.* New York: Warner Books, 1982.

Naisbitt, John, and Patricia Aburdene. *Megatrends 2000.* New York: Avon Books, 1990.

Pearce, Joseph Chilton. *Magical Child.* Toronto: Penguin Books, 1977.

Postman, Neil. *The Disappearance of Childhood.* New York: Vintage Books, 1982, 1994.

Reid, Angus. *Shakedown.* Toronto: Seal Books, 1997.

Rushkoff, Douglas. *Playing the Future: What We Can Learn from Digitial Kids.* New York: Harper Collins Publishers Inc., 1996.

Schneider, Cy. *Children's Television.* Lincolnwood: NTC Business Books, 1987.

Schwartz, Peter, Peter Leyden, and Joel Hyatt. *The Long Boom: A Vision for the Coming Age of Prosperity.* Cambridge, MA: Perseus Books, 1999.

Smith, J. Walker. *Rocking the Ages, The Yankelovich Report on Generational Marketing.* New York: HarperCollins, 1998.

Strauss, William, and Neil Howe. *Generations: The History of America's Future.* New York: Willliam Morrow, 1991.

Tapscott, Don. *Growing Up Digital: The Rise of the Net Generation.* Toronto: McGraw-Hill Ryerson, 1997.

Walsh, David. *Designer Kids.* Minneapolis: Deaconess Press, 1990.

Zollo, Peter. *Wise Up to Teens.* Ithaca, NY: New Strategist Publications, Inc., 1999.

Articles

"1999 Conference: Retailing to Kids and Teens." In *Kidscreen*, 1999.

Begley, Sharon. "Your Child's Brain." In *Newsweek*, February 19, 1996.

Digital Kids Report, The. Jupiter Communications, September 1996.

Journal of Social Issues, Winter 1999, Vol. 55, Issue 4.

Kaiser Family Foundation. *Kids & Media @ The New Millennium.* Fall 1999.

McNeal, James U. "Tapping the Three Kids' Markets." In *American Demographics*, April 1998, pp. 37–41.

McNeal, James U. "Born to Shop." In *American Demographics*, June 1993.

Minding the Set! Toronto: The Alliance for Children and Television/Rogers Cablesystems, 1994.

Naughton, Keith. "Can Toyota Get Its Mojo Back?" In *Newsweek*, January 17, 2000.

Neuborne, Ellen, and Kathleen Kerwin."Generation Y." In *Newsweek*, February 15, 1999, pp. 82–88.

"The New Teens." *Newsweek Special Edition*, Summer/Fall, 1997.

Roedder John, Deborah. "Consumer Socialization of Children: A Retrospective Look at 25 Years of Research." In *Journal of Consumer Research*, Chicago: University of Chicago Press, 1999.

"Secret Life of Teens, The." In *Newsweek*, May 10, 1999.

Statistics Canada. *General Social Survey on Time Use, 1998.*

Steinberg, Shawna. "Have Allowance, Will Transform Economy." In *Canadian Business*, May 13, 1998, pp. 59–68.

"Three Generations Living Together." In *Canadian Social Trends Summer '99 Report*, Statistics Canada, 1999.

Trends: The Canadian University in Profile. Ottawa: Association of Universities and Colleges of Canada, 1999.

"Under My Thumb?" In *Today's Parent*, March 1998.

Western International Media Corp. survey, 1998–99, *The Nag Factor: Parents, Nagging Kids and Purchase Decisions.*

Wolff, Michael. "Why Your Kids Know More About the Future Than You Do." In *New Yorker*, May 17, 1999, pp. 30–33.

Worzel, Richard. "The Future of Work—Getting Kids Ready." Trimark Investment Management Inc.

Index

MAY - - 2009